GREGORY DEXTER

120

120

Providence Town Meeting Records in Dexter's Handwriting, 1652

Gregory Dexter

of London and New England

1610 ~ 1700

By BRADFORD F. SWAN

1949 ROCHESTER · NEW YORK

THE PRINTING HOUSE OF LEO HART

THE PRINTERS' VALHALLA

THIS *is a series of books, published by The Printing House of Leo Hart of Rochester, New York, each of which is devoted to an individual whose career contributed to the development of bookmaking during the five hundred years since the invention of typography. It is hoped that the series, under the general editorship of George Parker Winship, will become a comprehensive, authoritative survey of the ways printing and its allied industries have attained their present position in the world. Present volumes in this series are:* DANIEL BERKELEY UPDIKE AND THE MERRYMOUNT PRESS, *by George Parker Winship;* ISAIAH THOMAS, PRINTER, PATRIOT AND PHILANTHROPIST, *by Clifford K. Shipton;* GREGORY DEXTER OF LONDON AND NEW ENGLAND, *by Bradford F. Swan; and* PETER SCHOEFFER OF GERNSHEIM AND MAINZ, *by Hellmut Lehmann-Haupt.*

To the memory of
MY FATHER
because he would have liked Gregory,
and to
MY MOTHER
because every book needs one reader
who is going to like it anyhow.

TABLE OF CONTENTS

LIST OF ILLUSTRATIONS

Page

LIST OF ILLUSTRATIONS

Unless otherwise indicated, all illustrations are from copies in the Library of the Rhode Island Historical Society.

INTRODUCTION

I have sought, in the pages which follow, to give some account of the life of Gregory Dexter. Perhaps I should say "lives," for, from the somewhat harassed position of the biographer, Gregory Dexter did lead two lives: one as a printer in London during the early years of the English Revolution and the other as a prominent figure in the young and struggling colony of Rhode Island and Providence Plantations.

In a sense these two careers split with almost crystalline precision along the line of cleavage marked by his crossing of the Atlantic Ocean. But since in this world the organic is never as rigidly exact in its behavior as the inorganic, the cleavage was not as neat and complete as it might have been. Thus I hope to be able to show that Dexter, in his last years in England, engaged in a sort of printing, much of it for Roger Williams, which turned his face toward New England. And, again, I hope that I have established, in my account of Dexter's first years in America, evidence of a brief return to his old trade, on this occasion in behalf of the press at Cambridge in New England, the first printer's shop in British America.

But, extending in opposite directions from these bridgeheads, lie the two principal parts of Dexter's career. That which runs back into the London printing trade will be, I trust, of interest to bibliographers and somewhat to students of English history, especially insofar as it is reflected in the activities of a London printer who worked on the side of the Parliamentary party. This section of the book must remain, perforce, rather specialized in its point of view, which is that of bibliographical examination. On the other hand, the second half of the book—that dealing with Dexter in Providence—is largely a matter of local history, to which I believe I have brought some new light, but which remains, nonetheless, another specialized field.

Consequently I fear lest bibliographers will be interested in only the first half of the book and will ignore the second, while those who approach it as American history will reverse that formula. Under the circumstances I can only point out that it was Gregory Dexter's life and he lived it; I have had to accept it as I found it.

I can also draw the bibliographical reader's attention to the fact that here is the story of what happened to a trained printer when he emigrated to a place where there was little or no use for the civilized skills that he possessed but where his general knowledge and education could be used to great advantage. And I can point out to the historical reader that here is the background of one man who almost instantly assumed a position of leadership in an American colony.

It is true that there have been moments, such as when I wrestled with a particularly knotty English bibliographical problem or tried to untangle the snarled land disputes of Providence Plantations, that left me wondering why I had to choose a biographical subject with such diverse interests—why I had to try to do two lives in one. But nonetheless I am happy to have had the chance to do it, for I have felt for a number of years that Gregory Dexter deserved some really serious attention from both *bibliographers and historians.*

For, you see, during his brief career as a London printer he turned out, I believe, some books of great importance to both England and America. On the other hand, in New England he was, for nearly 40 years, right-hand man to Roger Williams—something which will, I think, redound forever to his glory.

* * * *

This book, the reader will find, is often critical of the printed Catalogue of the Thomason Collection of 17th Century English imprints now in the British Museum. I have alternately leaned on the Catalogue and criticized it. In spite of my obvious debt to this source I have felt constrained to point out certain shortcomings in it, principally in the hope that by doing so I might emphasize the need for a modern revision of that work and plead my cause among Americans, to whom a revision would be of the greatest value. The fault I have found with the printed Catalogue will come as no news to scholars, who have long been aware of these deficiencies, but I can point out that, since this work was written under wartime conditions, when access to British collections was virtually impossible and to pester British scholars with questions would have been a thoughtless imposition, the difficulties of working with the Catalogue as it stands today were brought home to me with more severity than would normally be the case with the usual peacetime channels of communication open. In short, the inadequacies of the Catalogue, when it is unsupported by personal requests for addi-

tional information, are *sufficient to call for serious thought about a much-needed new edition, enriched with the wealth of bibliographical information which has been turned up in the years since its publication.*

In this work I have been assisted, counseled, and inspired by George Parker Winship. The book was his suggestion and he provided the unflagging interest which kept me at it; without him there just would have been no book.

I would also like to express my great debt to Lawrence C. Wroth, librarian of that most wonderful of libraries, the John Carter Brown. He has given me advice and assistance, and he and the two members of his staff, Miss Marion Adams and Miss Jeanette Black, have not only made available to me every resource of that institution but have also performed the indispensable service of listening with great patience whenever I wanted to "talk out" a problem.

To Peter A. Davidson, formerly assistant librarian at the Rhode Island Historical Society, and to his successor, Clifford P. Monahon, I am indebted for help in examining the excellent collection of Gregory Dexter imprints assembled by the late George L. Shepley and now in the Society's library.

I also wish to thank William A. Jackson, librarian of the Houghton Library, Harvard University, for his help with certain bibliographical questions.

Lastly I would like to thank my wife for her help which came in many forms—from making transcriptions and checking references to putting up with my frequent displays of bad temper when things went wrong.

BRADFORD F. SWAN

Providence, R. I.
June, 1946.

GREGORY DEXTER

I

AMONG THE MISTS

It was in 1637 that Gregory Dexter made his first documented bow to history, by helping William Prynne lose what was left of his ears.

Back of that date Dexter's career lies shrouded in the mists of time—the same time which, by entering into chemical combination with the vagaries of historians and bibliographers during the slow unrolling of three centuries, has produced a portrait that is less the likeness of a man than the hazy outline of a mythological character. From these mists Dexter emerges somewhat in the guise of a friendly spirit—not unlike the white god of a remote island tribe—who came from nowhere in particular, taught the inept Puritans how to print almanacs on their Cambridge press, and then disappeared into a convenient cloud.

But Gregory Dexter was no such myth; he was a very real man, a printer who could make the press a weapon and never hesitated to use it as such when a particularly domineering conscience told him that was the right thing to do.

He operated in London when the printing trade was in one of its more rebellious moods, fighting for the liberties of Englishmen as well as for its own freedom. In his brief London career, Gregory Dexter followed an extremely hazardous course, and it is small wonder that both his point of departure and his ultimate landfall are pricked on the chart in the shoals of the law.

But, however noteworthy his accomplishments as a printer, in such minor matters as vital statistics Gregory Dexter was most unsatisfactory. Genealogists who enjoy citing chapter and verse must content themselves with a tangle of vague assertions and untraceable claims which add up, at best, to the belief that he was born in England, possibly in Olney in the County of Buckinghamshire, in 1610, and that he died in Providence in New England, probably in 1700.

Although historians of the first New England press, since Isaiah Thomas, have seldom failed to mention a

Gregory Dexter and to give him credit for reviving the press in 1645 or 1646, after it had lain exhausted for half a decade from the labor of bringing forth the *Bay Psalm Book*, the increasing recovery of records concerning the man seems only to have confused writers, until some have even been reduced to offering the theory that there may have been two Gregory Dexters: the printer of London and the politician and preacher of Providence Plantations.[1]

It seems wise therefore, before proceeding with a biography of Gregory Dexter of London and Providence, to make sure that we are talking about one man and not two.

The proof that the London printer and the Providence inhabitant were identical is available, and to refute it seems nearly impossible.

On 8 September 1652, Roger Williams was in London trying to get a new charter for Rhode Island and Providence Plantations. That day he wrote a letter[2] to "my deare & faythfull friend Mr Gregory Dexter at Providence in New England," saying:

Jt hath pleased God Sr to ingage me in diuers Skirmishes agst ye Priests. both of Old & New England So yt I haue bene occationed (vsing the helpe of /printers/ Men vnknowne. to me) to Long for my old Friend. Sr it hath pleased God to hould open an open

---

[1] Lawrence C. Wroth flew this trial balloon in desperation when he was confronted by what appeared to him to be an irreconcilable conflict in the evidence. In "The Cambridge Press," an article contributed to *Bookmen's Holiday, Notes and Studies Written in Tribute to Harry Miller Lydenberg* (New York, 1943), he said:

"There is some faint uncertainty, however, as to whether this Gregory Dexter [the friend of Roger Williams] . . . . was after all a printer, whether he was in fact the Gregory Dexter of London who printed Milton's *Of Prelatical Episcopacy* in 1641 and Williams' *Key Into the Language of America* in 1643. We need not go into the conflict of dates responsible for our questioning this identity. But, if the two were one, that one did a remarkable feat of shuttling between his printing house in London and his farm in Providence."

George Parker Winship has also held that there might have been two Gregory Dexters, father and son. But since the problem raised by this hypothesis is more complex and brings in elements which will be discussed later, appraisal of the explanation which Winship offers will be postponed.

[2] *Early Records of the Town of Providence*, XV, 61-62. Hereafter the printed Providence records will be cited as *Prov. Recs.*

dore of preaching & printing wonderfully agst Romish & English
Will worships: At this present ye Deuill rageth & Clamours in
peticions & Remonstrances from ye Stationers & others to ye
parliamt & all crie shut up the presse The Stationers & others
haue put forth The Beacon fired: & The Second Beacon fired:
& Some Friends of yours haue put forth The *Beacon quenched*
not yet extant.

Sr Many Friends haue frequently with much Loue inquired
after you:...

...Diuers Friends of all Sorts here long to see You & wonder
You Come not ouer....

In another letter, written in 1669 to John Winthrop,
Jr., Roger Williams makes the flat statement that Gregory
Dexter "is an intelligent man, a master printer of London."[1]

The two letters, taken together, should dispel any
doubt that Gregory Dexter of London and Providence was
the London printer. It seems almost as though Williams
had posterity in mind when he interlined the word *printers*
in the London letter, and this same letter tells us not only
that Dexter had been a printer in London but that he had
been *the* London printer with whom Williams formerly
had done business, i.e., on his previous visit to England
in 1643-44. Its references to news of the printing trade
and its allusions to the prevailing attitude of the Stationers' Company are definitely aimed to give its reader
in far-off Providence the sort of gossip and shop-talk he
would be craving.

Friends are inquiring for him, Williams writes, and
wondering why he doesn't return to the pamphleteering
wars. In view of Dexter's character and career, this wonder
of his friends is not surprising; those reports of Beacons
Fired and Beacons Quenched must have left him nearly
overcome with nostalgia for the old London days.

* * *

S. C. Newman, a mid-19th Century genealogist of the
Gregory Dexter family, seems to have been the first to
advance Olney as the printer's birthplace. Unfortunately,
Newman gives not the slightest hint, either on his genealogi-

---

[1] *Narragansett Club Publications* (Providence, 1874), VI, 332.

cal chart, published in 1857, nor in his little book on the Dexter family, which came out two years later, as to where he got his information.[1] Nor is his claim for Olney strengthened by the fact that he placed the town in the wrong county, Northamptonshire. C. M. Banks, a skilled genealogist, lists Dexter as having been born in Olney, and gives the correct county, but his reference is only "Rhode Island Historical Society," which is unsatisfactory because it seems to take us right back to where we started from, to wit: Newman.

At any rate, before Newman, all writers who mentioned Dexter said he was born in London. The Rev. Morgan Edwards, itinerant historian of the Baptists, writing in the last half of the 18th Century, noted that Dexter "is said to have been born in London."[2]

The next oldest account, a manuscript genealogy dated 17 February 1819 and written by Jonathan Dexter, a great-great-grandson of the printer, states flatly that "Gregory Dexter was born in London."[3]

Whatever the merits of the respective claims, the matter was settled, so far as Rhode Islanders are concerned, when John O. Austin brought out his *Genealogical Dictionary of Rhode Island* (Albany, 1887). Austin cast his vote for Olney as the birthplace and 1610 as the birth date. The tremendous prestige of Austin's book will probably withstand any assault short of a parish register photostat, and even such a wary historian as the late Howard M. Chapin, who was a careful student of Dexter's career and the books he printed,

[1] The chart bears no title except the legend: *1610 DEXTER 1857* at top. Elsewhere on it is to be found the information that it was "Prepared and compiled by S. C. Newman . . . Providence . . . . . 1857." The book is *Dexter Genealogy: Being a Record of the Families Descended from Rev. Gregory Dexter. . . . . ,* by S. C. Newman, A. M. . . . . Providence: 1859. Newman's sketch of Dexter occupies pp. [7]-13. On p. 5 he states that Gregory Dexter was a cousin of Richard Dexter "who arrived in Boston in 1641. .."

[2] Morgan Edwards, "Materials for a History of the Baptists," in *Rhode Island Historical Society Collections*, VI, 321. Edwards' original manuscript is in the library of the Rhode Island Historical Society. All references here to the history will be to the printed version, to be cited hereafter as: Edwards, *History.*

[3] Rhode Island Historical Society Manuscripts, VII, 146.

hedged only so far as to write that Dexter "*is said* to have been born at Olney, Northamptonshire, England in 1610."[1]

The date of 1610 for Dexter's birth receives some support from Morgan Edwards, who wrote that Dexter died in "—— about the 91st year of his age." Although Edwards left blank either the year or the place of Dexter's death, he did note in his manuscript that Dexter and two other Baptist ministers of Providence ordained the Rev. James Clark as minister of the Baptist church at Newport in 1697, thus showing that Dexter was alive and active as late as that year.

Furthermore, a legal document shows that Dexter was living in 1699, and, lastly, there is the evidence that Dexter was made free of the Stationers' Company in 1639. It would not have been strange for him to have taken up his freedom at the age of 29; that would be, in fact, a likely age for such an event.

Newman gives the date of Dexter's death as 1700, which is consistent if he combined Edwards' information as to age with his own as to birth date. Here Austin, it may be added, follows Newman again.

All this may seem like needless winnowing of a few unimportant dates, but it has not been indulged in as a purely cerebral exercise nor from any desire to disparage earlier biographers. The simple fact is that so much which is dubious has been placed on the record in regard to Gregory Dexter that a critical appraisal, of such scant evidence as we have, seemed in order.

II

A PRINTING JOB FOR PRYNNE

ALONG ABOUT Eastertime in 1637 a man named Nathaniel Wickens came surreptitiously to the printing shop in Newgate Market where Gregory Dexter worked. Wickens wanted a printing job done for his master, William Prynne, the Puritan pamphleteer.

[1] *R. I. H. S. Collections*, XII, No. 4 (October, 1919), p. 105. Italics in the quotation are mine.

Prynne was supposedly confined to the Tower for life, the poorer by £5000 and part of his ears, for having written *Histrio-Mastix*, a diatribe against stage plays, the publication of which was so unfortunately timed that the book went on sale at Michael Sparkes' shop, at the sign of the Blue Bible in Green Arbour, in Little Old Bailey, just a few weeks after Charles' queen, Henrietta, had been taking part in some amateur theatricals at court.

Prynne and Archbishop Laud had been engaged in a theological feud for some time, with the prelate having none the best of it until *Histrio-Mastix* made its untimely appearance. After that, however, the tide of battle ran very distinctly in Laud's favor and little was said in the Star Chamber in Prynne's behalf when life imprisonment in the Tower was recommended.

But, imprisoning Prynne and silencing Prynne were two different things. The Tower proved no bar to his publishing activities and he promptly set about writing and issuing three more books which aroused Laud to further action before the Star Chamber.[1] But even this threat of more punishment failed to deter Prynne when he thought the time had come to push another Puritan pamphlet through the press.

Just why Prynne or his man Wickens chose the shop where Dexter worked, aside from its convenience in being near Wickens' home, is hard to say. But one theory would be that since the shop was probably that of a widow, Elizabeth Purslow, operated by her in behalf of her young son Thomas since the death of her husband, George Purslow, master printer, in 1632, the establishment might be lacking in strict supervision and its employes open to inducements.

Dexter and one William Taylor were working at the shop, probably as apprentices, although it is possible that

---

[1] The books were *A Looking-Glasse for all Lordly Prelates, Newes from Ipswich*, and *The Vnbishoping of Timothy And Titus*. For further information on Prynne's literary activities about this time, see Ethyn Williams Kirby, *William Prynne: A Study in Puritanism* (Cambridge, 1931), pp. 20-50; and Samuel Rawson Gardiner, editor, *Documents Relating to the Proceedings Against William Prynne in 1634 and 1637 . . . .* (Westminster, 1877).

they had already completed their terms.[1] Whatever their status, it is not likely that they were cold toward this opportunity to pick up a bit of money, and, although it could be argued that even at such an early age Gregory Dexter stood ready to strike a blow against oppression, in the form of Archbishop Laud, the lure of the 30 or 40 shillings promised by Prynne seems a much more logical reason for his undertaking the first printing which we can attribute definitely to him: *Instructions to Church Wardens*.[2]

Actually, three persons were indicted, so to speak, for the printing of this inflammatory tract, which was designed to teach Puritan church wardens how best to thwart visitations, inspections, and other unwelcome manifestations of the long arm of the Episcopacy; young Tom Purslow was also named in the original charge or "articles" of the Commissioners for Ecclesiastical Causes.

But Dexter and Taylor, in their replies to the articles, make no mention of Purslow, although they admit their

---

[1] Determining the exact status of the two printers at this date is difficult. Dexter refers to the place as his "master's house," and Taylor uses the term "fellow-servant" in describing Dexter. But the indefiniteness of these terms is obvious. The one concrete fact we have to go by is that neither had yet been admitted to the Stationers' Company.

Edward Arber, in his introduction to Vol. I of *A Transcript of the Registers of the Company of Stationers of London: 1554-1640* (London, 1875-1894), hereafter cited as Arber, *Transcript*, states that freedom of a City Company followed upon an apprenticeship of not less than seven years, and that, in 1556, the term of service was not to end before the apprentice's 25th year of age. But he is not clear as to whether an apprentice became free of the Company immediately upon completion of his term, nor does he say whether the customs had changed any by 1630. English bibliographers have not chosen to be specific about this procedure but the best information that I have been able to get from American authorities is that it would be the general rule for a printer to be admitted to the Stationers' Company as soon as he finished his apprenticeship, provided he was 24 and had the necessary fees. For this opinion I am indebted to William A. Jackson, librarian of the Houghton Library, Harvard University, and American secretary of the Bibliographical Society of London.

[2] No copy of this book is known. I have taken the title from the Calendar of State Papers. Mrs. Kirby, in her book on Prynne, prefixed a *Briefe* to this title, but she informs me that she never saw a copy of the book.

7

own and one another's parts in the escapade. Nor has any reply from Purslow come down to us—if he ever was called upon to make one.

The chances are that he was quickly cleared. He may have been involved only on a sort of technicality, as will presently appear, and his youth may have saved him even from questioning. For, in the Spring of 1636, only a year earlier, when a list of the master printers of London and their partners was drawn up, the Purslow establishment was listed to "Master George Purslow his widdow: her sonne is about 18 (or 17, or 14) yeares old (at most:)."[1] Yet, in the Star Chamber Decree of 11 July 1637, Thomas Purslowe is one of the 20 master printers allowed to have a press.[2] That Thomas Purslow would be given the coveted privilege of owning a press within a couple of months of having been suspected of actual participation in subversive printing is just too far-fetched to merit serious consideration. We must assume, therefore, that he was held in no way to blame for *Instructions to Church Wardens*.[3]

Mention has been made of a technicality in Purslow's case. This requires some explanation, which, although it may not pertain directly to Dexter, presents an interesting puzzle in London printing trade customs of the time.

Thomas Purslow was the son of a master printer, and sons of master printers could be admitted to the Stationers' Company by patrimony, although not until they reached the age of 24. On the other hand, there is evidence that

---

[1] Arber, *Transcript*, III, 704. Arber explains there that the parenthetical matter is of a later date.

[2] Ibid, IV, 532.

[3] There seems to be no foundation for the assertion by H. R. Plomer in *A Short History of English Printing, 1476-1898* (London, 1900), p. 175, that "for printing this [the *Instructions*] and other books, Thomas Purslowe, Gregory Dexter, and William Taylor of Christchurch were struck from the list of master printers." Paradoxically, Thomas Purslow's name appears in the Star Chamber list of master printers within a month or so of the incident. Furthermore, when the case came up none of the three had even been admitted to the Stationers' Company—to say nothing of being master printers. Nor does a thorough search of the Arber *Transcript* show either the slightest support for Plomer's statement or any other similar names which might have led Plomer to say that *a* Dexter, *a* Purslow, and *a* Taylor were censured.

A

DECLARATION

FROM BOTH

HOUSES

OF

PARLIAMENT,

With the Additionall Reasons laſt
preſented to his M A I E S T Y.

Sabbathi 12. *Martii* 1641.

Ordered by the Lords and Commons in Parliament
aſſembled, that the Declaration with the additio-
nall Reaſons laſt preſented to his Majeſty, ſhall be
forthwith Printed and publiſhed.

Jo. Brown Clerick. Parl.
H. Elſine. Cler. Parl. D. Com.

Whereunto is annexed, His Maieſties S P E E C H to the
Committe, the 9 of *March*, 1 6 4 1. when they preſented the DECLARATION of both Houſes of *Par-*
liament at *New-maket.*

London, Printed by *R. Oulton* & *G. Dexter*. 1 6 4 1.

Title; A Declaration from Both Houses of Parliament

A
DECLARATION
TO HIS
MAIESTY.

May it pleafe your moft
excellent Majefty,

Lthough the expreſſions of your
Majeſties Meſſage, the fecond of
this inſtant Moneth, doe give juſt
caufe of forrow to Us your Majeſties *faithfull* Subjeɑts, the Lords
and Commons in *Parliament;* yet
it is not without fome mixture of
Confidence and Hope, confider-
ing they proceed from the Mifap-
prehenſions of our Aɑions and
Intentions, which having no ground of *truth* or *reallity,*
may, by your Majeſties Juſtice and VVifdome be removed,
when your Majeſty ſhall be fully informed, that thefe
feares and *jealouſies* of Ours, which your Majeſty thinks to
be Caufeleſſe, and without juſt grounds, doe neceſſarily
and clearly arife from thefe dangers and diſtempers, into
which the mifchievous and evill Councellors about you
have brought this Kingdome: and that thofe other *feares*
and *jealouſies* by which your favour, your Royall prefence
and Confidence have bin withdrawn from your *Parlia-*
ment, have no foundation or fubfiftence in any Aɑion, In-
tention, or Mifcarriage of Ours, but are meerly grounded
upon the falfhood and malice of thofe, who for the fup-
porting and fomenting their own wicked defignes againſt
the

Text; A Declaration from Both Houses of Parliament

widows were neither admitted to the Company nor were they eligible for admission.[1] Arber shows that about this date the Purslow establishment was part of a chain of printing shops owned, or at least controlled, by the three most powerful figures in the trade: Miles Flesher, John Haviland, and Robert Young.

If this was the case, it might account for Thomas Purslow being some sort of nominal head of the establishment, in view of his patrimony right, and for Flesher, Haviland, and Young seeing to it that the shop kept its right to have a press when the presses were being apportioned by the Star Chamber.

On the other hand, it should be stated that Elizabeth Purslow used her name in the shop's imprints at this time and did so from 1633 until 1644, when Thomas Purslow's name appears on *Romes Ruine*, by Daniel Featley, done for Nicholas Bourne, who had long been the shop's best customer.[2]

With Thomas Purslow eliminated, Dexter and Taylor, who described themselves as both "of Christ Church parish, London," and as "printer" and "stationer," respectively, are left as the principals in this secret printing affair. And by their own testimony it would seem that the chief responsibility was Dexter's.

The story is told with relative completeness in three documents which have survived in the Public Record Office and are summarized in the *Calendar of State Papers, Domestic Series, . . . 1637.* These are the "articles," i.e., the charges, brought by the Commissioners for Ecclesiastical Causes, and the replies of Dexter and Taylor.

---

[1] Arber, *Transcript*, III, 701.

[2] This corrects the statement in R.B. McKerrow, *A Dictionary of Printers and Booksellers in England, Scotland & Ireland . . . .1557-1640* (London, 1910), p. 222, that Thomas Purslow's "name is not known to appear in any imprint." On 19 April 1646, however, *Perfume Against the Sulpherous Stinke of the Snuff of the Light for Smoak, called Novello-Mastix,* by John Saltmarsh, bears Elizabeth Purslow's name, and so does *Christian Liberty Vindicated,* by John Mayer, which was printed for Matthew Welbancke in 1647. Query: Did Thomas Purslow die young, and the business revert to his mother? The work will be cited hereafter as: McKerrow, *Dictionary.*

At their examination, which probably took place in May, 1637, Purslow, Dexter, and Taylor, described as "printers or stationers," were charged with having printed or published "a scandalous pamphlet or epistle thereunto" which was shown to them at the hearing. They were "exhorted to declare how many of them they printed, how much each of them composed, who brought the same to them to set, and what had become of the original" copy.

Actually, there were two offenses involved: the printing of the pamphlet of instructions, and the printing of the epistle "thereunto."

The charge alleged that "about two years since they printed in their master's house some sheets of paper called 'Instructions to Churchwardens, &c.,' of which many copies were dispersed in several places in London by them or with their consent."

As for this charge, both Dexter and Taylor admitted the printing but said that it had taken place some four to six weeks before Easter, rather than two years earlier, and both denied circulating the books. They both said that Dexter had carried them, sealed up in "cap paper," to Wickens' house where Prynne was to pick them up, and Dexter said he didn't know what became of them after that. Perhaps someone else had done a previous printing of the book, for Dexter testified that Prynne had sent him what he described as "a little book" in a sealed letter, asking him to print it "as privately as he could." The Dexter-Taylor edition of the tract was 1000 copies, according to their testimony.

Their next assignment was to print an epistle for this book. According to Dexter, about Easter Wickens came to the shop with the copy in a sealed package. An accompanying letter, Dexter testified, was directed to him from Prynne, telling him to print the enclosed copy and he would give Dexter and Taylor "very good content."

Taylor said he was shown the letter and the copy by Dexter, who told him they would be well paid for printing it. The two men forthwith printed the eight-page epistle, with Dexter doing all the composition, according to Taylor. A thousand copies of one four-page part were run off, they testified, and 500 of the other four pages. The reason for this difference in the press-run is not apparent.

As soon as they had finished one perfect proof Dexter threw the original copy into the fire, according to his own testimony; he had been directed by Prynne's letter to take this precaution.

Another precautionary step marked this secret printing. The day after he brought the copy, Wickens showed up at the shop with a closely sealed packet which contained an initial letter C. Carved in boxwood—Taylor described it as "very curiously cut," and "a very complete letter, the best examinant ever saw"—it served a two-fold purpose. In the first place, it was a brand new letter, and hence unknown among the printers of London.[1] Secondly, it added sting to Prynne's tract for, if turned in one direction, it revealed a pope's head, and, turned the other way, it showed "an army of men and soldiers."

The examiners were most anxious to find out what had become of this letter C, but they got little satisfaction from Dexter, who said he had not even noticed its tricky properties and did not know who had it, although he believed it had been returned to Prynne sealed up. Taylor likewise didn't know what had become of it.

The initial C had been provided for use in the "scandalous epistle" and hence should be the criterion in determining whether a copy of *Instructions to Church Wardens* is one of the Dexter-Taylor edition or belongs to the earlier printing.

It was not long before Wickens was knocking again at the door "hard by the press." He wanted Dexter to bring a proof of the epistle to the Wickens' home—his father was a cheese-monger in Newgate Market—and meet Prynne there so that the author could check the proof.

Dexter admitted keeping the rendezvous. He arrived first and went into an inner room. Prynne showed up for the meeting in company with his keeper, discipline at the Tower evidently being very lax in his case. The pamphleteer immediately went into the room where Dexter was

[1] This indicates that the printers themselves were able to identify one another's ornamental initial letters readily.

waiting, while the Wickenses went about luring the keeper upstairs. They argued that it would be unwise for him to be seen in the open shop, but the real reason for their maneuver was to get the keeper where he couldn't see Dexter when the latter left the conference.

One or two minor phrases in Taylor's testimony, which, strangely, was not given until 14 November 1637, merit attention. He says that Wickens used the shop's back door, "to which he was appointed by Dexter to come," and that "after some little parley Dexter went forth and stayed about half an hour." He presumed, he said, that Dexter had gone to the meeting with Prynne at the nearby Wickens' home.

An especially interesting part of Dexter's testimony is his contention that the epistle was for a "book which examinant never saw." Apparently Dexter did not connect the epistle with the *Instructions* he had printed some four to six weeks earlier.

What the upshot of the whole case was, so far as the printers were concerned, we do not know. No further action against them appears on the record, and perhaps the authorities were satisfied that their testimony had clinched the case against Prynne, who promptly lost the rest of his ears and was subjected to other severe punishments and fines.

Perhaps the explanation lies in the "Notes for the Journeymen Printers" which Sir John Lambe, the prelates' watch dog of the press, issued on 14 June 1637.[1] In this document Sir John blames seditious printing on the trade practice of hiring "foreigners" instead of giving qualified journeymen employment. He observed that no seditious pamphlet had been printed but what some journeymen printers had been "the directors therein." He infers this was a result of the master printers employing "foreigners" in preference to journeymen, which left the journeymen unemployed. He went on to suggest that "those that are honest men and serve their full time might so far be provided for that neither the King's printer nor any other printer should employ foreigners so long as a freeman is

[1] *Calendar of State Papers, Domestic Series, ... 1637*, p. 214.

unemployed." In conclusion he observed that this would also be a means of uncovering "sinister printers and printing."

Of course it is not certain that Dexter, Taylor, and Purslow escaped punishment in this case, but whatever happened to them it did not retard their progress in their profession for long. William Taylor was made free of the Stationers' Company on 13 November 1637—incidentally, the day before the date of his deposition in the case, indicating a relation between his admission and his past sins. Gregory Dexter took up his freedom on 18 December 1639, and Thomas Purslow did the same on 2 March 1640 (/41).[1]

III

THE BACKGROUND OF A PARTNER

IF THE authorities meted out no punishment to the printers of *Instructions to Church Wardens*, they had ample precedent for their course of action. Four years earlier, when Michael Sparks, the bookseller, had brought out William Prynne's *Histrio-Mastix*, Sparks had been fined £500 and forced to stand in the pillory while the hangman publicly burned the book under his nose. But even the Star Chamber's most enthusiastic moralists had exculpated the actual printers of the book. Lord Cottington, whose pronouncement on Prynne, Sparks, and Buckner, the hapless licenser, seems to have set the pace for sentences in this case, recommended the acquittal of the printers, and Lord Heath also acquitted them, "noething being proved against them."[2]

The records of the Star Chamber name three printers in this case: Allde, Jones, and Cotes. The imprint of *Histrio-Mastix* bears only the initials E. A. and W. I., however.

[1] Arber, *Transcript*, III, 688.

[2] Samuel Rawson Gardiner, editor, *Documents Relating to the Proceedings Against William Prynne in 1634 and 1637...* (Westminster, 1877), pp. 17-21. Secretary Windebancke concurred in this opinion. In the poll of Star Chamber members these three men were the only ones to mention the printers. There was, incidentally, considerable difference of opinion as to Sparks' sentence.

These would stand for Elizabeth Allde and William Jones, for, although the exact date of Edward Allde's death is uncertain, Elizabeth was a widow as early as 1630 when, on 12 November, she was described as such in a list of master printers contributing to the repair of St. Paul's Cathedral.[1]

The Allde printing plant was an old established firm. It dated back to John Alday, one of the printers enrolled in the Charter of the Stationers' Company in 1556, who did business at the Long Shop in the Poultry.[2] The shop came into the hands of his widow, Margaret, and his son, Edward, in 1584, Edward having been admitted to the Stationers' Company on 15 February 1584 (i.e., 1585) "by patronage." Mother and son ran the business jointly until about 1589, when Edward Allde set up another press at the Gilded Cup in Fore Street, Cripplegate, and began handling printing there for the trade.[3] Margaret Allde continued to run the shop in the Poultry alone, taking apprentices from 1593 to 1600, until she finally sold out a few years later.

The actual travel of the ownership of a printing shop and the theoretical rights in it were two different things, however, and accordingly we must regard the John Alday business as having passed to Edward Allde by 1590. Edward Allde's first book entry at Stationers' Hall is found in the Registers under the date of 1 August 1586.[4] According to McKerrow's *Dictionary*, "his earlier work consisted chiefly of ballads, but in later days he is found printing the works of Thomas Churchyard, Samuel Daniel, Thomas Dekker, Christopher Marlowe, John Taylor the water poet, and many other noted writers. In character his printing differed little from that of his father, but his later books were printed throughout in Roman letter and he favored quarto rather than smaller sizes. In 1597 the Company of Stationers

[1] She gave £10. See H. R. Plomer, "S. Paul's Cathedral and Its Bookselling Tenants," in *The Library* (New Series), III, 261-270.

[2] Henry R. Plomer, *A Short History of English Printing, 1476-1898* (London, 1900), pp. 101 and 163.

[3] McKerrow, *Dictionary*, pp. 5-6. See also R. B. McKerrow, "Edward Allde As A Typical Trade Printer," in *The Library*, 4th Series, Vol. X, No. 2 (Sept., 1929), pp. 121-162, with reproductions of Allde's ornaments.

[4] Arber, *Transcript*, II, 450; III, 702.

seized his press and letters, which had been used in printing a Popish confession, and forbade him to print; but the Archbishop of Canterbury afterwards authorized the Company to allow him to resume his trade. He was again in trouble in 1599 and with several others was mentioned in an order of the Master and Wardens against printing certain books that had been condemned and ordered to be burnt. (Arber, *Transcript*, III, 677-678.)"

Allde had moved his shop frequently; by 1597 he was at Aldersgate, "over against the Pump," and in 1604 he was "upon Lambert Hill, near Old Fish-street." The establishment finally came to rest by 1615 "near Christ-Church," on Newgate Street.[1] It was this Newgate Street shop which passed to Elizabeth Allde on the death of her husband. She operated it there until 1640, although after 1632 the problems of management were undoubtedly the responsibility of her step-son, Richard Oulton.[2]

Richard Oulton was related to Mrs. Allde in some way; the designation as step-son is an arbitrary choice from among several possibilities.

Mrs. Allde is termed Oulton's mother-in-law in the Stationers' Register[3] when, on 22 April 1640, he entered for himself 21 titles "which lately did belong to Mistris Aldee his mother in law deceased."[4] But elsewhere in the

[1] McKerrow, *Dictionary*, p. 5; Plomer, *Dictionary of Booksellers and Printers 1641 to 1667* (London, 1907), p. 142.

[2] The subject of widows operating printing plants will bear examination. There are numerous instances of this situation and, apparently, no attempt to analyze them has been made.

[3] Arber, *Transcript*, IV, 507.

[4] The titles were: *Guy of Warwick, Sir Philip Sidney's OURANIA** (by N. B.), *The Christians Morning and Evening Sacrifice** by Doctor Collett, Bradford's *Meditacions, Treasury of Hidden Secretts,* Godly Graces, The Gardeners Laborinth, Grafting and Planting, Cavalarici the English Horseman** (by G. Markham), *Naturall and artificiall Conclusions, The Owle** a play, *A Book of Cookery, LEAR and his 3. daughters,* REYNOLD the ffox, ffrier BACON and ffrier BUNGEY,* ffrier RUSH, ROBIN HOOD and litle JOHN,* ffrier and the Boy, Beware the Catt, Like to Like. Quoth the divell to the Collier, The rate of Expences.*
Of these books, those marked with an asterisk had been assigned to Master Allde by the estate of Mistress White, plus a number of others. Immediately after Oulton entered these titles he assigned all right and title in *The Christians Morning and Evening Sacrifice* to John Benson.

same record Oulton is referred to as her son by a former husband.[1] This reference, a list of master printers and their partners, dated approximately in the Spring of 1636, states:

> Master Edward Aldee: his widdow (dead) habet filius. 28: admititur filius: (ye master and company know little of him. Olton is her sonne by ye former [husband])[2]

Giving an exact translation of this document's Latin is a task, but it would seem to mean that Edward Allde's widow had a son 28 years old and that the son had been admitted to the Company. In 1636 this would have fitted Oulton exactly, for he had been admitted to the Company, presumably by patrimony, in 1632, and the required age for such admission was 24.

Thus this would be a satisfactory explanation of a complicated set of facts, were it not for another reference which complicates the situation even further. Another, earlier, list of "such as keepe printing-houses" states:

> Mistris Alde widdowe of Edward Alde [who] deceased about 10 yeares since, (but she keepes her trade by her sonne, who was Ra[lph] ioyners sonne) neuer Admitted, neither [? is she] capable of Admittance:[3]

Careful study of these puzzling data will reveal only that they cannot all be correct; there are conflicts everywhere. Whoever contributed the section on Elizabeth Allde to McKerrow's *Dictionary* solved the problem by giving her a son by a first marriage to Ralph Joyner. This son, also Ralph by name and probably the one who was admitted to the Company in 1633, is, according to the *Dictionary*, supposed to have carried on the business for her for a number of years, and Oulton enters the picture by marrying one of her daughters. The objection to this theory is

---

[1] Arber, *Transcript*, III, 704.

[2] The portions in parentheses were added at a later date. The *husband* was apparently inserted by Arber.

[3] Arber, *Transcript*, III, 701. Date of this list is about 1634. The portion in parentheses was added at a later date; that in square brackets was added by Arber. One Raphell Joyner was admitted to the Stationers' Company on 6 May 1633. [*Transcript*, III, 687.]

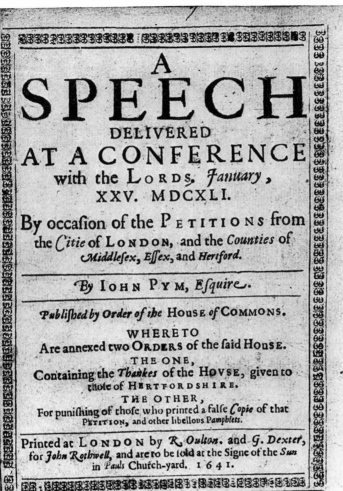

A SPEECH

DELIVERED
AT A CONFERENCE
with the LORDS, *January*,
XXV. MDCXLI.

By occasion of the PETITIONS from
the *Citie* of LONDON, and the *Counties* of
Middlesex, Essex, and *Hertford.*

By IOHN PYM, *Esquire.*

Published by Order of the HOUSE *of* COMMONS.

WHERETO
Are annexed two ORDERS of the said HOUSE.

THE ONE,
Containing the *Thankes* of the HOVSE, given to
those of HERTFORDSHIRE.

THE OTHER,
For punishing of those who printed a false *Copie* of that
PETITION, and other libellous *Pamphlets.*

Printed at LONDON by R. Oulton. and G. Dexter,
for *John Rothwell,* and are to be sold at the Signe of the *Sun*
in *Pauls* Church-yard. 1641.

Title; A Speech by John Pym at a Conference with the Lords

1

JANUARY 25.
1641.

At a *Conference* betwixt both *Houses*, concerning divers *Petitions* presented to the *House* of *Commons*: M^r PYM appointed to manage that CONFERENCE.

My LORDS,

 Am commanded by the *Knights*, *Citizens*, and *Burgesses* assembled for the *Commons* in *Parliament*, to present to your *Lordships* divers *Petitions*, which they have received from severall parts concerning the *State* of the *Kingdome*: whereunto they are chiefly moved by that constant *Affection*, which they have alwayes exprest, of maintaining a firme *union* and good *correspondence* with your *Lordships*; wherein they have ever found much *advantage*, and *contentment*; but never held it more important & necessary, then at this time, wherein the *Wisdome* and *Resolution* of *Parliament*, have as many great *Dangers* and *Difficulties* to passe through, as ever heretofore.

A 2

We

2

Text; A Speech by John Pym at a Conference with the Lords

that it would give a modern meaning to the term "mother-in-law," a meaning which would be extremely doubtful in the 17th Century.

On the other hand, there is the statement that Oulton is the son by the former marriage. And, thirdly, there is the evidence that he was not a son but a step-son.

Obviously, no two of these conditions agree.

But whatever Oulton's relation to the Allde family, he took over the shop and began doing business for himself there as early as 15 April 1633, when he entered his first book at Stationers' Hall: *Markes or noe markes of the Kingdome of heaven or a treatise of things necessary (or) unnecessary to the kingdome of GOD*, by Henry Greenwood.

He had been made free of the Company on 15 February 1632, and there could be no better proof of his prominent position in the trade than his rapid rise in its ranks. He was clothed, which is to say that he was admitted to the Livery, comprised of master printers, on 29 March 1638, at the largest renewal of the Livery at any one time since 1 July 1598. Oulton and 16 others made the grade that day. He was probably only 30 years old at the time.

On 28 June 1636, Oulton entered at Stationers' Hall *The Famous and Worthy History of GUY Earle of WARWICK*, a poem by John Carpenter, and in the period from 1638 to 1640 he was one of several printers engaged in turning out quartos of plays, "very poorly printed," according to Plomer.

Some time after 11 August 1640, the date on which it was preached, Oulton published *New Fort of True Honour Made Impregnable*, a sermon by Samuel Kem, in a pamphlet of 27 pages.

Evidently he had had some success with Carpenter's poem on Guy of Warwick for, on 24 November 1640, "Master Oulton" entered at Stationers' Hall *The True Story of Guy, Earle of Warwicke*, in prose, by Martyn Parker.

But the 1640 title bearing Oulton's imprint which is of most interest in the present study is Richard Montagu's θεανθρωπικου *Seu De Vita Jesu Christi Domini Nostri Originum Ecclesiasticarum Pars Posterior*. This 517-page book bears the following imprint:

17

Londini, Typis R. Olton & Eliz. Purslow, & prostant venales apud Jos. Kirton & Tho. Warren sub signo Equi albi, in Coemeterio Paulino. M.DC.XL.

The collaboration of the shops of Richard Oulton and the Widow Purslow in this printing offers us an explanation of how Oulton and Dexter met, if the proximity of their two shops in the Newgate district were not reason enough. It would be perfectly normal for Dexter, whose ability as a compositor was attested by his hasty job for Prynne, to be a prominent workman, if not the actual foreman, in the Purslow establishment, and it would be just as natural for him to strike up an acquaintance with Oulton during consultations on the project.

It would have been one way for a young printer, either just made free of the Stationers' Company or just about to become a freeman, to come to the attention of a young master printer who had recently taken over some 21 "copyrights" and undoubtedly would be looking for a smart young hand.

In any study of this sort a guess has to be made somewhere, and it is mine that it was during the printing of Bishop Montagu's work that Dexter and Oulton met and made the connection which was to lead, in the following year, to formation of the printing house of R. Oulton & G. Dexter.

IV

R. O. & G. D.

THE FIRST printing known to us which bears the names of both Richard Oulton and Gregory Dexter is John Milton's *Of Prelatical Episcopacy*, issued, according to the catalogue of the Thomason Collection in the British Museum, in July, 1641.

Choosing a more prophetic title for the new printing firm's first work would be difficult. With this blast at the rule of the prelates the press of Richard Oulton and Gregory Dexter sounded the keynote for a brief but prolific career as printers of pamphlets aimed at upholding the hand of the Parliament in its struggle against Church and King. With such a start, it can hardly be said that their output became increasingly vigorous in opposing the forces arrayed against English liberties, but by and large the course indicated by this, their first product, was to be their course for the duration of their joint career.

Although their names do not appear on it, Oulton and Dexter, or Oulton alone, had issued a month earlier, that is, in June, 1641, another Milton tract: *Of Reformation Touching Church-Discipline in England: And the Causes that Hitherto Have Hindered It.* The pamphlet can be attributed to the Oulton press on the basis of a block initial A on its first page, an identifying block in that what was once the letter E in its decorative scheme has been altered with the chisel to an I.[1]

Earlier in 1641 a number of less important works had issued from Oulton's press, with only his name in the imprint; whether Dexter helped in producing these we cannot say.

On 16 March 1640/1, Francis Rous had made a speech to Parliament, and John Wright, Jr., bookseller at the King's Head in Old Bailey, brought it out in a quarto tract of eight pages: *A Speech Made Before The Lords In The Vpper House.* It bears no printer's name but the ornamentation indicates that it came from Oulton's press. In the same format and probably issued about the same time was *Two Speeches by Sir Beniamin Rudyard Concerning The Palatinate*, printed for Francis Constable, whose shop at the time was in Westminster Hall. Here again our only clue to the printer is the ornaments used.

Oulton put his name on two single sheets which came out in March 1640/1, according to the Thomason Catalogue. The first was *A Psalme of Thanksgiving to be sung by the Children of Christs Hospitall on Monday in the Easter Holy-dayes at S. Maries Spittle*, and bore the musical notation. The other single sheet had the same title except for a change of the date from Monday to Tuesday.

---

[1] The Yale Library, which has four copies of this pamphlet, reports that three are variants. All copies, however, seem to bear the misspelling "Freind" on the title-page.

Two other pamphlets which came out about this time, probably in April and May, bore the name of Oulton only.

These were the first of several commissions for John Bartlett, senior, a London bookseller whose shop at the Gilt Cup near St. Austine's Gate dealt largely in theological works. Bartlett was an ancient foe of Laud, and had suffered from the prelate's persecution, having spent several months in prison after incurring the Archbishop's displeasure in December, 1637.

Probably the first of the series was John Geree's *Vindiciae Voti*, 36 pages. That it preceded the same author's *Judahs Joy at the Oath*, which the Thomason Catalogue says came out in May, 1641, is most likely, since *Judahs Joy at the Oath* also containes "a briefe answer to the Protestation Protested," which was the sub-title of *Vindiciae Voti*.

Socinianisme Confuted, by George Walker, a book of 370 pages, was the next printing which Oulton's plant did for Bartlett. The imprint mentions Oulton only.

There is no imprint on a little 12-page quarto pamphlet, *Sir Henry Vane His Speech* (of) *June 11. 1641*, except the notation that it was done for Francis Constable. Here again we must rely on the ornaments for our ascription. And the ornaments are our sole clue to the printer of *Sir William Parkins Speech To The House of Commons* (on 5 July 1641); in this case the work does not bear even the name of the bookseller.

In this group of Richard Oulton imprints the last is *Dutie of Sir Francis Worthy delineated in his commiseration of the sorrowes and sufferings of the Lady Elizabeth Queen of Bohemia*, done for an unidentifiable F.W. The Thomason Catalogue assigns this to July, 1641.

With the appearance of the Milton pamphlet in July the firm of Richard Oulton and Gregory Dexter was definitely in business. Their principal trade was in the printing of small quarto tracts, pamphlets, broadsides, and similar material, unimposing in form and size and generally undistinguished as either typography or presswork.

Their products give the impression of having been put through the press in great haste, that they might reach the booksellers' stalls before the news they contained had grown stale. And that is exactly what most of them were designed to do. Oulton and Dexter were not turning out "press books"; they were printing news pamphlets— propaganda pamphlets, if you wish—and their primary object, as in many modern newspapers, was speed in production.

The Long Parliament had begun to sit, London was in a political turmoil, and one petition after another was being presented to Parliament. On the other hand the Parliament was just as frequently issuing declarations on this or that, and its members were making speeches which even the slow communication channels of that day recognized as newsworthy. Every bookseller in the trade, regardless of his political or ecclesiastical sentiments, was on his toes to rush this news to an eagerly waiting public.

It is not strange that, in this era, newspapers began to appear. But the pamphlets which men like Oulton and Dexter printed were the fore-runners of these newspapers. Hence it would be as foolish to criticize them on aesthetic grounds as it would to hold a modern election "extra" up to ridicule for its typographical shortcomings.

One interesting aspect of the works which issued from the Oulton and Dexter shop at this time is that not one of those which does not state specifically that it was done for some bookseller or publisher was ever entered by the printers at Stationers' Hall as their property.

But this is what we might expect. Who cared about copyright at a time like that? As well copyright the "race final" edition of a modern newspaper. Once the news was published it had little value to anyone. The right to reprint meant little or nothing. The man who got his edition up for sale first probably cared little who brought out the second edition—and generally no one ever did.

The whole problem of entrance, license, and publication is complicated. The most recent writer on the subject, W. W. Greg, states that the percentage of books entered to books printed was about 60, or "probably in the neighborhood of two-thirds."[1]

[1] W. W. Greg, "Entrance, Licence, and Publication," in *The Library*, XXV, Nos. 1 & 2 (July-Sept., 1944), pp. 4 ff.

That is far from the proportion which prevailed in the case of Oulton and Dexter. Of some 74 pieces which I have ascribed to them and which were produced prior to 24 June 1643, the date of the order of Commons for all news books and pamphlets to be entered in the hall book and to bear the name of printer and publisher, only two were entered, in both cases by the bookseller for whom they were printed. This would be about three percent, instead of 60 or more.

This does not necessarily upset Greg's figure, however, for he was talking about the overall picture, and we, in discussing Oulton and Dexter's business, are considering a highly specialized form of product. As we have said, there was little copyright value attached to this type of product; once the books had "hit the street" it was all over. Literature, on the other hand, was something else again. Here the reprint rights were jealously guarded, even as they are today.

There is still another reason for the discrepancy between Greg's proportion and that shown in this study. We must keep in mind the fact that many of these pamphlets might well have caused trouble for those responsible for them and hence would naturally be cloaked in anonymity. An attempt to break this secrecy was, of course, the reason behind the Parliamentary decree of 24 June 1643.

Some time in 1641, the partners brought out a theological work of some size, 201 pages, for John Bartlett. This was *The Great Oracle*, by Francis Rous. There was probably only one edition, although this shows two variant title-pages.

Late in the year, probably not long after it was delivered, Oulton and Dexter printed for Richard Lownes *The Substance of Mr. Pymms Speech (of) Novemb. 9. 1641*. Their names are not on the piece, which must be identified as their work through its ornaments. It is but one sheet, folded in quarto.

Another product in this series, and one of particular interest because the Thomason Catalogue describes it as "probably a forgery," is *Sir Arthur Haslerigg His Speech in Parliament*, a reply to the charges of high treason brought on 4 January 1641/2 by King Charles against Haslerigg, Lord Kimbolton, Pym, Hampden, Stroud, and Hollis.

Just why the Catalogue's compiler suspected it of being a forgery is hard to say. It was done for F. C. and T. B., probably Francis Cowles and Thomas Banks, and although it bears no printer's name it is easily identified by the old Allde ornament on the title-page, an ornament which occurs in at least a half-dozen other Oulton and Dexter imprints both of this period and of later date. The title-page date, MDCXLII, is less easily explained, except as a simple typographical error; it hardly seems likely that the speech would not have been printed before late March or early April.

The last of this series of anonymously printed tracts which are assigned to Oulton and Dexter on the basis of the ornaments is *Mr. Whites Speech in Parliament on Munday, the 17th of January*. Only six pages, it was produced for F. Coules and T. Bancks. Francis Cowles, a bookseller in Old Bailey, was often associated with Thomas Bates in the publication of ballads, but for this venture he joined with his neighbor, Thomas Banks, a publisher of theological tracts, among them some of those written by the Rev. John Cotton in his controversy with Roger Williams over liberty of conscience.

The Thomason Catalogue assigns the date of 22 January 1642 to *A Message of Thanks delivered to the Lords Commissioners for Scotland by Mr. Pym, from the House of Commons*. It was done by R. O. & G. D. for William Larnar, the noted Puritan and Independent bookseller whose shop was then at the Sign of the Bible in East Cheap.

Larnar was quite a character and may well have had an effect on Gregory Dexter's life and thought. The bookseller himself later served in the Parliamentary army. He is suspected of having had a part in the operating of the notorious Coleman Street Press in 1643, and Plomer says he helped the Overtons, Robert and Richard, among others, to print books secretly.

It is just a series of coincidences, and adding them up may produce almost any result the adder desires, but Morgan Edwards wrote that Dexter was in "the stationery business...in company with one Coleman, who became the subject of a farce called 'The Cutter of Coleman

Street.' " This farce was, of course, Abraham Cowley's famous play. Although the Cowley play offers no hint that it was actually written about Oulton, the fact that Edwards mentions it cannot be brushed aside; the allusion would be simply crazy if it weren't true.

The Coleman Street Press was famed for faking imprints of the Oxford Press after King Charles had set up his court in that university town on 29 October 1642. Again it may be just a coincidence, but Oulton and Dexter possessed and used a decorative device which was actually the bogus Oxford University Press seal.[1]

Admittedly this evidence is too nebulous to tie Oulton and Dexter to the Coleman Street Press—there could be a dozen other interpretations or explanations of the few facts—but nevertheless it is a tantalizing thought and one which might bear further investigation where the working material is available.

V

TRICKS OF THE TRADE

ONE OF the practices indulged in by Oulton and Dexter to speed up production was to incorporate type which had been used in one book in a second, without changing it— "lifting," the practice would be called today.

Shortly after 25 January 1641/2, the date of the matter which it contains, there appeared *A True Copie of the Masterpiece of all those Petitions which have formerly beene presented by the Major, Aldermen, and the rest of the Common Counsell of the Citie of London*. Done for J. B., initials which may stand for John Bull, bookseller in Grub Street who suddenly reappeared in business in 1640, after a long period of inactivity, and began publishing political pamphlets and broadsides, this little tract of 10 pages contains two petitions from the London city officials. One of them starts on the recto of leaf A3, misnumbered as page 4.

[1] R. B. McKerrow, *Printers' & Publishers' Devices in England and Scotland, 1485-1640* (London, 1913), lists as his #338 the fake Oxford coat-of-arms which is to be found on several Oulton and Dexter imprints.

TO THE
HONOURABLE
THE
KNIGHTS, CITIZENS
and *BURGESSES*, of the Houſe
of COMMONS aſſembled in
PARLIAMENT.

The humble Petition and Anſwer of the Major,
Aldermen, and the reſt of the Common Councell of
the Citie of LONDON.

Sheweth,

Hat the Committee of this Honourable
Houſe upon Saturday the 22.of this inſtant
Ianuary, ſent a meſſage to the Petitioners
for the loane of one hundred thouſand
pounds, or of ſo much thereof as could
conveniently be forthwith raiſed, for levying of forces to ſuppreſſe the Rebells in *Ireland;* To
which Meſſage ſomething was then anſwered, and a
further anſwer in writing promiſed.

In

Text; A True Copie of the Masterpiece of . . . . Petitions

TO THE
HONOURABLE
THE
KNIGHTS, CITIZENS
and BURGESSES, of the House
of COMMONS assembled in
PARLIAMENT:

*The humble Petition and Answer of the Major,
Aldermen, and the rest of the Common Councell of
the Citie of* LONDON.

Sheweth,

THat the Committee of this Honourable House upon Saturday the 22. of this instant *January*, sent a message to the Petitioners for the loane of one hundred thousand pounds, or of so much thereof as could conveniently be forthwith raised for levying of forces to suppresse the Rebells in *Ireland*, To which Message something was then answered, and a further answer in writing promised.

In

Text; A Speech by John Pym

This entire page of type, even to the ornamental head-piece, was picked up intact and used without change as the page numbered 3 in *A Speech Delivered At a Conference with the Lords. January XXV. MDCXLI.*, by John Pym. This edition of Pym's speech was printed for John Rothwell, at the sign of the Sun in Paul's Churchyard, who entered it at Stationers' Hall on 29 January 1641/2.

The dates given in the Thomason Catalogue do not help us in fixing the exact date of issue of each of these pamphlets. Since each one deals with an event which took place on 25 January 1641/2, and the fact is so stated on each title-page, the printed Thomason Catalogue, as is its wont, assigns to both the date of 25 January.

Regardless of the exact dates of issue or of the relative order of appearance, the fact remains that Oulton and Dexter saw fit to pick up a whole page of type used in one book for one bookseller and to use it all over again in another book for another bookseller.

Furthermore, they used part of this type on this same page—the caption heading, down through the words: "The humble Petition. . .," or seven and a half lines of type— in a third pamphlet: *Two Petitions of the Knights, Gentlemen, Freeholders, and others of the Inhabitants of the County of Hertford.*

Now, although these petitions were delivered to Parliament on 25 January 1641/2, the imprint states that this book was "Printed by a perfect Copie by R. O. & G. Dexter, and are to be sold by John Sweeting at the signe of the Angell in Popes Head Alley, 1642."

The interesting feature here is the date 1642, in the imprint. It is hard to believe that a page of type would be left standing in the Oulton and Dexter shop for two months. Since the Thomason Collection does not include a copy of the *Two Petitions of Hertford*, we can get no help from that quarter.

On the face of this typographical evidence we can conclude that probably the *Masterpiece of all those Petitions* and *Pym's Speech of January 25, 1641* came out somewhat later than their assumed date and that the *Two Petitions of Hertford*, following them, appeared near enough to the beginning of the new year on 25 March to make it advisable to date it forward in the imprint. The only other explanation would be that the 1642 is a simple typographical error and that all three books appeared shortly after 25 January, an assumption which would be in line with the fact that Rothwell entered *Pym's Speech* in the Stationers' Registers on 29 January.

Some support for either theory can be found in the fact that an even smaller portion of this caption heading, four lines this time—starting with "Knights, Citizens..." and ending with "...in Parliament."—was used on p. 1 of *A True Copie of the Petition of the Gentlewomen and Tradesmens-wives...*, covering an event which took place on 4 February 1641/2. This last-mentioned book, a small quarto of eight pages, was done, incidentally, for John Bull, and is dated 1641. Certainly, although the relative order of the first two books cannot be stated definitely, there is no doubt that the *Two Petitions of Hertford* followed them and preceded the *Petition of the Gentlewomen and Tradesmens-wives*.

Whether this same segment of type appears in any other works from the Oulton and Dexter press at this period I cannot say, since I have been unable to examine any other copies of contemporary titles. But I can state that the heading had been completely re-set by the time the *Petition of Cornwall*, of 22 April, was printed.

On 26 January 1641/2 the "humble Petition of the Young-men, Apprentices, and Sea-men, in and about the Citie of London" was presented to the House of Peers and was printed for William Larnar by Oulton and Dexter. Here again the imprint bears the date 1642 but it seems hard to believe that this is not an error—whether deliberate or not, I hesitate to say—for the item is a broadside, or single-sheet. Since the Thomason Catalogue does not list it, and thus provides no evidence to the contrary, I have placed it first, chronologically, among the surviving Oulton and Dexter broadsides.

The next Oulton and Dexter product was another broadside, *The humble Petition of 15000. poore labouring men, known by the name of Porters....*, printed for John Bull. The Thomason Catalogue dates it 31 January 1642 (i.e., 1641/2) and the only clue in the imprint is the date 1641.

Petitions were the main stock-in-trade of printers in those days, and some time in January Oulton and Dexter brought out, for Samuel Enderby, bookseller at the sign of the Starre in Popes Head Alley, *Three Petitions unto Parliament. The first by the County of Surrey to the House of Lords....* Also ascribed to January by the Thomason Catalogue is *Certaine Observations concerning the Duty of Love*, by Thomas Devenish, done for Larnar.

But the printers continued to do political tracts of a newsy nature, and soon issued *Six Great Matters of Note* for F. Cowles. The Thomason Catalogue dates this as 2 February 1641/2, which is a good example of its dubious value in establishing dates of issue. The fifth "matter of note" listed on the title-page is "His Majesties Message to the House of Commons. February 7. 1641," but the cataloguer elected to choose 2 February because that was the date of two petitions of the Lords and Commons to the King which are also included in the pamphlet.

Of much greater interest to us, however, is the way in which Oulton and Dexter re-issued this pamphlet, with a new title, *Seaven Great Matters of Note*, when additional material appeared in the form of a petition from the "Courtiers, Citizens, Gentlemens and Trades-mens wives." For this second pamphlet, also done for Cowles, is a good example of the practices of such high-speed production as was known in those days.

For this new issue Oulton and Dexter simply changed *Six* to *Seaven* in the first line of the title-page and replaced an ornamental device in the lower half of the page with an additional explanatory sub-title, starting: "ALSO the humble petition of many thousands of Courtiers Citizens Gentlemens and Trades-mens wives..." Then they proceeded to print the additional text matter in very small type on the verso of the title-page, a space which had been blank in the earlier pamphlet. The imposition was otherwise unchanged, and by these few shifts and additions the printers were able to provide Cowles with a pamphlet in which the news had been brought up to date.

The remainder of the Oulton and Dexter output for 1641 was rather routine. When the silk throsters presented their "very considerable and lamentable petition" to Commons on 12 February 1641/2, Oulton and Dexter printed it as a broadside and possibly as their own venture, since no bookseller's name appears on it. If this was so they were showing their true feelings as anti-prelatical printers, for the petition prayed "that the Prelacy may be totally Abolished" and that "Voteing of the Popish Lords removed out of the House of Peers."

There followed *A True relation of certain passages which Captaine Basset brought from Cornwall, 13, Feb....*, done for John Bull; *An Ordinance from His Majesty and Parliament for the Ordering of the Militia of England and Wales*, printed for Cowles and dated 15 February by the Thomason Catalogue; and *Certaine Reasons presented to the King's Majestie by Parliament touching the Princes stay at Hampton Court. Also the Parliament's Answere to a message from the Scotch Commissioners....*, printed for John Wright and dated 24 February by the Thomason Catalogue.

No date more definite than February is assigned by the Thomason Catalogue to the broadside *Petition of Kent*, which likewise bears no publisher's name and may have been another of the printers' private ventures. Another product which reveals no bookseller's name is *The Cry of a Stone*, a tract against excessive Separation, i.e., the Brownists, by Robert Coachman. The Thomason Catalogue assigns it to February.

Foure Matters of High Concernment is another news pamphlet, done for Cowles and Banks. A small quarto of only eight pages, it is one of several books done by Oulton and Dexter which bear the bogus Oxford seal. This is dated 2 March by the Thomason Catalogue, but only on the basis of the fact that it contains "Questions resolved upon by both Houses March 2," according to the text.

Our two printers resorted to their trick of "lifting" type already set and used when they printed two Parliamentary declarations in rapid succession some time in March 1641/2. *A Declaration From Both Houses of Parliament* was ordered by the two houses on 12 March to be "forthwith printed and published." On 23 March another declaration was made, and it was printed by Oulton and Dexter as *Another Declaration From Both Houses of Parliament: Sent to His Majesty, March 23. 1641.*

For the second title-page the *A* was simply pushed to the left and *NOTHER* in small capitals added to it. The next three lines—*Declaration / From Both / Houses*—were picked up intact, with the single change of the *T* in *Declaration*, it having been the wrong size (too small) in both the title-page and the caption heading on p. 1 of the earlier pamphlet.

Therefore, if we can rely on "forthwith" in the Parliamentary order meaning what it says, and both pamphlets came out about the same time after the events they describe, then type was left standing in our printers' shop for as long as 10 days or two weeks.

There is one more aspect of bibliographical interest to the first *Declaration*. The copy in the Shepley Collection at the Rhode Island Historical Society is uncut. Its pages measure about 7-5/8 by 5-3/4 inches, and since the format is quarto, this gives us a paper size of 15-1/4 by 11-1/4 inches.

Paper of approximately this same length[1] was used by Oulton and Dexter to print their broadside *A True Coppy of the Petition of the Lord Maior, Aldermen, and the rest of the Common Councell of London....*, which, like the other two pieces, was apparently done by the printers as their own venture. All three, incidentally, bear the date 1641, which, if true, means that *Another Declaration* was done within two

---

[1] Although the top and both sides of the copy examined have been trimmed, the sheet measures 15¼ by 10½ inches. This paper bears an unidentifiable watermark of the "columns" style, with the initials A over B between the columns and a cluster of small balls above the A. None of the watermarks on the broadsides I have examined can be identified by examples in the standard works on the subject. All of them, however, are of the style prevailing in the period. The paper used for the petition of the Silk Throsters is notable for its size; although it bears a pot, it measures 15 by 11⅜ inches even after top, bottom and one side have been trimmed. This pot watermark, which has the pot surmounted by a conventionalized crown, which is surmounted in turn by a crescent, bears the initials A D. Another paper, which was printed upon in 1643, measures 15¾ by 10⅙ with all edges trimmed; it bears a crown-crested coat-of-arms which is not clear enough to be identified with exactitude. Other papers are marked with bunches of grapes.

days of the news it covered. The broadside, according to internal evidence, was printed later than 18 March, although the petition itself was delivered in February; probably the presentation of a similar petition on 18 March had served as a spur to the publication of both papers.

Probably it was during March that *Further Intelligence from Ireland*, based on a letter dated there 11 March from Capt. Muschampe, captain of the Castle of Cork, was printed by Oulton and Dexter for Henry Overton, a bookseller whose shop at the entrance to Popes Head Alley was to handle many of our printers' books in the next year or two.

Several other books printed by Oulton and Dexter bear the year 1641 on their title-pages, although no more definite date than that can be assigned to them. They are: *News From Heaven Both Good and True Concerning England*, collected by E. F.; *A Rot Amongst the Bishops, or a Terrible Tempest in the Sea of Canterbury....*, a satire in verse by Thomas Stirry, which is embellished with four wood-cuts; *Napiers Narration*, a commentary on the Book of Revelation, which was done for Giles Calvert at the Black Spread Eagle in St. Paul's Churchyard, official printer under Cromwell and publisher of much early Quaker literature; and *A Coppy of a Letter of Mr. Cotton*, which is ascribed to Oulton and Dexter on the basis of the ornaments used.

Thus, by the end of 1641, Gregory Dexter had printed his first piece of controversial theological literature emanating from New England and had made his acquaintance with the writings of the Rev. John Cotton, the Boston divine and pamphleteering opponent of Roger Williams.

One cannot help but wonder whether Gregory Dexter had any thought of the future as he set these sentences on the first and second pages of Cotton's book:

"...It is true, one *Sheba* of *Bickry* blew a Trumpet of such a seditious Separation; I meane, one Mr. *Williams* late Teacher of *Salem*, but himselfe and others that followed stiffely in that way, who were all excommunicated out of the Church and banished out of the Commonwealth...."

VI

A BUSY YEAR

On the basis of the number of works which have been preserved to us, 1642 was much the busiest year of the Oulton and Dexter partnership. Many of their 1642 products are ephemeral pamphlets and single-sheets, but at least the printers were engaged steadily in producing things of this sort from March to the middle of September.

Then a gap appears during which only two items were produced, so far as we know—one a broadside dated as of 7 November by the Thomason Catalogue and the other John Taylor's *An Humble Desired Union betweene Prerogative and Priviledge*, which bears only Oulton's name in the imprint. It was not until 24 December that another book appeared with an imprint indicating it was their joint product.

It is true that some time before the end of the year, i.e., 24 March 1642/3, they brought out a book of nearly 500 pages, John Goodwin's *Imputatio Fidei*, with a preface dated 24 January, and that two other books which might be too large to be considered pamphlets came off their presses before the year's end. Nonetheless this seems hardly enough production to have kept the shop busy through the apparent gap from September to late December, and the presence, part way through this period of seeming inactivity, of a work bearing the name of Oulton alone, indicates that Dexter may have been temporarily absent.

Roger Williams refers to Dexter, in a letter to John Whipple, Jr., [1] as a man "versed in militaries." If Williams means by this phrase that Dexter had had military experience—had been a soldier, in other words—there appears to be no other period in his English career than these months in 1642 when he would have had a chance to serve with the army.

It is possible that Dexter served a short hitch with the Parliamentary forces in the Fall of 1642, leaving his job in

[1] The letter, dated at Providence, 8 July 1669, is printed in *Narragansett Club Publications*, VI, 327.

London for a brief spell as did other printers, notably his friend William Larnar.

This is, of course, only speculation. But it is difficult to see where else Dexter could have become "versed in militaries." Certainly he had no military experience in Providence, that we know of, and Williams would hardly have felt it necessary to call the fact to Whipple's attention if the experience had been gained in Whipple's own community. It is of further interest to note that Williams coupled the military knowledge with the assertion that Dexter was "a man of education, and of a noble calling" (i.e., a printer).

Oulton and Dexter opened the year 1642 by issuing *A Discourse tending to prove the Baptisme in or under the defection of Antichrist to be the Ordinance of Jesus Christ*, by P. B. (i.e., Praise-God Bare-bone.) It was a small affair, 40 pages, and came out in March, according to the Thomason Catalogue, although the title-page bears the date 1642. Since no publisher is named it may have been one of the printers' own ventures.

Also assigned to March, 1642, by the Thomason Catalogue is *New Lambeth Fayre*, by Richard Overton, an antipapacy poem of 14 pages. No publisher is named in the imprint, but it is possible that it was printed for the author.

On 22 April a petition from the inhabitants of Cornwall was presented to Commons, and Oulton and Dexter printed it, probably soon after that date, for John Bartlett. Similarly the printers put out in broadside form for John Frank a petition to the King from the people of York, presented to His Majesty at York on 30 April and "desiring a happy union betwixt the King and the Parliament."

Some time after 19 May our printers brought out, for F. C., probably Francis Cowles, *A Remonstrance Or The Declaration of the State of the Kingdome*, a statement from the Lords and Commons. Another York petition, this one from "many thousands of faithfull and peaceably affected Subjects" to the King, was printed by Oulton and Dexter for Benjamin Allen, in May, according to the Thomason Catalogue. The only date on the broadside itself is "... delivered...on Thursday last," which indicates that the

TO THE
HONOURABLE
KNIGHTS, CITIZENS
and *BURGESSES*, of the House
of COMMONS affembled in
PARLIAMENT.

The moft humble PETITION of the
GENTLEWOMEN, TRADESMENS-WIVES,
and many others of the *Female Sex*, all Inhabitants of the Citie of LONDON, and
the Suburbs thereof.

With leweft fubmiffion fhewing,

THAT we alfo with all thankfull hu-
mility acknowledging the unwearied
paines. care and great charge, befides
hazard of health and life, which you
the noble worthies of this honourable and renowned Affembly have un-
dergone, for the fafety both of *Church*
and *Common wealth*, for a long time already paft; for
which not only we your humble Petitioners, and all
well affected in this Kingdome, but alfo all other good
Chriftians

Text; A Copie of the Gentlewomen's Petition

Die Martis 25. *Januar.* 1641.

I T is this day Ordered by the Commons House of Parliament, that Master Speaker, in the Name of the House, shall give thanks unto Mr Pym for his so well performing the service hee was imployed in by the Commands of this House at this Conference. And it is further Ordered, that Mr Pym be desired to put the Speech hee made at this Conference into Writing, and to deliver it into the House, to the end that it may be printed.

H. Elsynge *Cler. Parl. D. Com.*

Text; *A Speech by John Pym*

printing followed closely upon the date of the event it describes. Allen, the publisher, had his shop at the Crown, in Pope's Head Alley, where he brought out much of the political and theological literature of the period, including several New England tracts, as we shall see. Frank, for whom the earlier York broadside petition was done, had his shop next door to the King's Head Tavern in Fleet Street and was a well known publisher of political broadsides.

For Allen and John Bull our printers did *The Petitions of Northampton-shire and Oxford-shire*, to which I cannot ascribe a date; the pamphlet, only one sheet folded in quarto, is not in the Thomason Collection. It is of peculiar interest to me because the title-page has a border of quad fleurons, a favorite ornament with Oulton and Dexter and one which keeps recurring throughout their work. Also issued in May, according to the Thomason Catalogue, was a 168-page book, *The Fulnesse of Gods Grace in Christ*, by Francis Duke. The Thomason copy bears the MS. notation: "written by the Cooke of Hell at Westminster." No publisher is mentioned.

It was for Larnar that the printers did the broadside *The humble Repromission and Resolution of the Captaines and Souldiers of the Trained Bands, and other Inhabitants of the County of Essex*. The repromission, presented to the trained bands at Dunmow 10 June 1642 "...was within three days after, subscribed by ten Thousand Hands." Hence it could not have come out before 13 June, although the Thomason Catalogue, following its practice of using the date of an event described, assigns it to 10 June.

No publisher is named in *A True Relation of the Taking of Mountjoy in the County of Tyrone by Collonell Clotworthy. 26 June*. The pamphlet probably did not come out before mid-July, at the earliest.

Assigned to June by the Thomason Catalogue is *The Peasants Price of Spirituall Liberty*, by Nathaniel Homes, a 77-page book done for Benjamin Allen. Another example of the practice of the printed Thomason Catalogue in dating the issue of certain pamphlets is *A Relation of the Proceedings of our Army in Ireland since 10 June to this present*

July, also done for Allen. The Catalogue dates this as 10 June, ignoring "this present July."

The name of another bookseller appears in our record when Oulton and Dexter brought out *July 5, 1642 Two Declarations*, for Joseph Hunscott, the beadle of the Stationers' Company and on occasion printer to the Long Parliament, an energetic fellow in ferreting out secret presses.

A definite date, that of 7 July, can be given to *A Most True Relation Of A Wonderfull Victory it pleased God To give those two Worthy Commanders Sir Robert and Sir William Stuart*, also printed for Hunscott, at the order of Parliament. The full date appears in the imprint.

Two more Oulton and Dexter imprints, both single-sheets and done apparently as private ventures of the printers, are ascribed to July by the Thomason Catalogue, although one of them, *True Newes from Somersetshire* [respecting the proceedings of the Commission of Array] *25 to 29 July*, could hardly have appeared before the end of the month. The other broadside is *A True Relation of Lord Brookes setling of the Militia in Warwickshire*.

Like these two items, neither *Some Special Passages from Hull, Anlaby and Yorke truly informed* nor the broadside *A Letter to the Kingdome to stand upon their Watch least the darke Winter nights, by the lighting of Cannons prove terrible to their spirits* contains any mention of publisher or bookseller. The Thomason Catalogue assigns the former to 1 August and the latter to 3 August.

Also assigned to 3 August is a book of considerable interest to us: *A Modest and Cleare Answer to Mr. Balls Discourse of set formes of Prayer*, by John Cotton. This was printed for Henry Overton in Pope's Head Alley and contains 56 pages. This is the second Cotton item to be printed by Oulton and Dexter.

An example of how confusing the Thomason Catalogue can be in fixing dates of issue is offered by *Two Letters The One from the Lord Digby To The Queens Majestie: The Other From Mr. Thomas Elliot, to the Lord Digby*. Digby's letter is dated 10 March, and hence the pamphlet appears in the Thomason Catalogue under that date. But Elliot's letter is dated 27 May, and the catalogue also lists the pamphlet under *that* date. Thirdly, the title-page shows that Parliament on 1 August ordered the matter to be printed. But, of final importance is the printed date *August. 5.* in the upper right-hand corner of the title-page, indicating how long after the Parliamentary order the printing was done.

This criticism of the Thomason Catalogue's dating method is presented here to emphasize what is stated in its preface, that the titles are "arranged, as far as possible, according to the dates of the events which they record," and that the collector's famous practice of dating his acquisitions is made use of only "*in the case of books or pamphlets not referring to any special event.*"[1]

The *Two Letters* was printed for John Bartlett. Benjamin Allen was the publisher of *An Extract of Letters, wherein is related certaine remarkable passages from Yorke and Hull,* dated 5 August by the Thomason Catalogue. This was followed, about 13 August, by *An Advertisement to the Kingdome of England to consider their present dangers,* a piece favoring Parliament. It bears no publisher's name. Stephen Bowtell, at the Bible in Pope's Head Alley, was publisher of *A True Relation of how the Isle of Wight was secured, in August,* which, the title would indicate, did not come out until after the end of the month. Bowtell, who dealt mainly in political material and some Americana, brought out *The Simple Cobbler of Aggawam* in 1647.

Instructions Agreed upon By the Lords and Commons…for The Deputy Lieutenants for the County of [blank] is an interesting pamphlet. Oulton and Dexter printed it for Henry Overton, who entered it at Stationers' Hall on 7 September 1642. The Thomason Catalogue, apparently using the collector's date, assigns it to 15 September. Since this is one of the rare cases in which an Oulton and Dexter imprint was entered on the Stationers' Register, it affords an opportunity to compare date of entry with date of issue. If Thomason's date is accurate, Overton must have entered the copy rather than the printed book. On the other hand, the entry title seems to follow exactly the title of the printed

[1] Italics are mine.

book, something which is by no means always the case in such comparisons. The entry title states that these instructions are for the County of Suffolke. In the printed title there is a blank space to be filled in with the name of the county. The Shepley copy, now in the Rhode Island Historical Society, has been filled in, in a contemporary hand: "Lincolne and every other prticuler Countie." There is also a blank for the name of the county in the text on p. 2, but in the Shepley copy, this has not been filled in. The Shepley copy, incidentally, is uncut and measures 8 by 5-3/4 inches.

One might wonder why a book of this sort would be entered in the Registers. The answer seems to be that it was strictly a commercial proposition, and one in which the bookseller wished to be sure that no one else brought out an edition before his was published, thereby ruining a venture which obviously had a limited, specific market.

Strangely, the next printing that we know of in Oulton and Dexter's career was a broadside done *for* them, according to the Thomason Catalogue. It was an order of the Commons authorizing the Lord Mayor to search the houses of strangers and persons disaffected to the Parliament, and is given the date 7 November 1642 by the Thomason Catalogue. If the description in the catalogue is correct and the broadside was done *for* instead of *by* our printers, it may be taken as further evidence of Dexter's absence from the shop at this time. On 8 December, according to Thomason's dating, John Taylor's *An Humble Desired Union betweene Prerogative and Priviledge* appeared, printed by R. O. only.

An Ordinance by Parliament, for the Preservation of the Westerne Parts of the Kingdome, dated 24 December in the Thomason Catalogue, was the work of both printers, and was done for Henry Overton. Also published by Overton, at some unknown date, was *The Answer of the Deputie Lieutenants of the Countie of Devon. To The Declaration of Sir Ralph Hopton and other his trayterous Adherents that have lately . . . invaded the said countie*. Not even the year is given in the imprint of this work, and Thomason had no copy of it, but the Shepley copy, in the Rhode Island Historical

Society, has 1642 written in a contemporary hand on the title-page margin.

For Andrew Crooke, at the Green Dragon in St. Paul's Churchyard, one of the foremost publishers of the day, Oulton and Dexter printed John Goodwin's *Imputatio Fidei; or, a Treatise of Justification.* This had an engraved title-page and portrait of the author, and thus was, typographically speaking, quite a cut above their usual product.

However, I am sure collectors would much prefer an humbler product of the Oulton and Dexter shop: *New Englands First Fruits.* This little book, which appeared on 31 January 1642/3, according to Thomason, was the first of the so-called Eliot Indian Tracts and the first known book which relates to Harvard College.[1]

The book was printed for Henry Overton and was another connection of the printers with the field of New England books. The men for whom they printed were going more and more into the New England market, and the printers were thus becoming more widely known to New England authors and to those who brought manuscripts from the American colony to be printed in London. The fact that Dexter worked on this book may have been one of the reasons that Roger Williams sought him out the following September, when he arrived in England with the manuscript of his book on the Indian language.

Some time during 1642 Oulton and Dexter also printed for Henry Overton *The Churches Resurrection,* by John Cotton. This book has a feature in its title-page decoration—the

---

[1] There were, apparently, three variants of this edition. One, probably the first, contains a final signature of only two leaves, printed by half-sheet imposition. Another contains a final signature of four leaves, D_3 being occupied by a small list of errata, while D_4 is said to have been a blank. The Church copy was of this latter type, but lacked the final blank. The corrections called for in the list of errata have not been made in the other copies. This would seem to indicate that the errors were noted during the press run, the errata list was put into type, and the final forme re-imposed, thus providing a gathering of four leaves which was used in certain copies. A third variant is implied by the Church Catalogue which states that certain mistakes in pagination, present in both the first variant and the copies containing the errata list, have been corrected "in some copies."

use of border ornaments to make up a sort of device—which will, from now on, become an increasingly frequent practice of both printers and, eventually, of Dexter alone.

The year 1642 closed, so far as I have been able to trace the evidence of the printing, with the issuance of *The Last Weeks Proceedings of the Lord Brooke*, dated 1 March by the Thomason Catalogue.

VII

DEXTER ON HIS OWN

THE PRINTING done by Oulton and Dexter in the early part of 1643 differs considerably from that of their preceding years; it included more books and fewer pamphlets.

William Greenhill preached a sermon to Parliament on 26 April 1643, using Matthew III, 10, as his text. Greenhill appointed Benjamin Allen to print it, and Allen turned the job over to Oulton and Dexter who brought it out for him in a book of 50 pages entitled *The Axe at the Root*. Physically the most noteworthy element of the work was its use of four crowned ornaments to form a decorative device for the title-page. This practice becomes an increasingly frequent one with Dexter, as we shall see.

Shortly after 4 May Oulton and Dexter printed a folio broadside, measuring at least 16 by 10 1/2 inches, for John Wright: *A Declaration and Motive of the Persons trusted, usualfy*[1] *meeting at Salters Hall in Breadstreet, to all well affected persons in the several Parishes within London, and the parts adjacent, for Contributing the Value of a Meale weekly, towards the forming of some Regiments of Voluntiers, to be payd during these times of Danger.* These broadsides were apparently designed to be distributed to appointed collectors in various parishes or precincts, for there is a blank space in one line to be filled in with the name of the parish or precinct. The broadside is, of course, very pro-Parliament, since the Sub-Committee for Volunteers which issued it was raising regiments "as

[1] The letter, which should be an *l*, is either a broken *f* or a broken long *s*.

Auxiliaries to the Trained Bands, and to be used for defence of Parliament, Citie, and parts adjacent, as occasion shall require."

Although it is not identified in the imprint as their work, *Englands Covenant Proved Lawfull & Necessary*, by S. C., preacher at B. F., is decorated with two devices and an initial letter which appear in many other works by Oulton and Dexter and hence it can be ascribed to them. A 16-page pamphlet, it was printed for Henry Overton.

Oulton's name alone appears in the imprint of *A Remonstrance Presented to the High and Mighty Lords the States of Zealand*. The imprint also states that this pamphlet, which consisted of only one sheet folded in quarto, was printed on 29 May 1643, five days after the date of the Parliamentary order empowering Rous, Reynolds, and Pym to have it printed if they saw fit.

The date of this pamphlet has generally been regarded as marking the end of the Oulton and Dexter partnership, but, if the date of 15 June which the Thomason Catalogue assigns to *Church-Government and Church-Covenant Discussed* is accurate, at least one issue of that book appeared with the initials of the two printers in its imprint after their supposed parting. But the physical nature of *Church-Government and Church-Covenant Discussed* would enable one to theorize that it might have been printed several weeks before it appeared. The book is in three parts, the first having been printed by Oulton and Dexter and the second and third by T. P. and M. S., probably Thomas Paine and Matthew Simmons. The initials of the latter two printers do not appear on the general title-page, but are on the title-pages of both "An Apologie" and "An Answer." It could have been possible for some of the sheets in a collaborative printing such as this to have been delayed, thus holding up the issuance of the whole book although the general title-page had been done before the partners parted.

Of course, on the other hand, Thomason's date may have been in error, or he may have picked up a copy of the second issue, for there were two. One carries this imprint: "Printed by R. O. and G. D. for Benjamin Allen, Anno Dom. 1643." In the other the words "and are to be sold at his Shop in Popes head-Ally, 1643" have been added, the "Anno Dom." having been deleted.

This book was another item in the Oulton and Dexter list of New Englandiana. The preface "To the Reader" was signed by H. Peter, believed to be the Rev. Hugh Peter, formerly of Massachusetts Bay, while the Rev. Richard Mather has been credited with authorship of the text.

What became of Richard Oulton after May, 1643? There is no readily available evidence that he continued in the printing business. Many of the old Allde ornaments passed to Dexter, and so, apparently, did the type. No less than five of the ornaments which McKerrow found in books printed by Edward Allde and which were used by Oulton and Dexter in their joint operations appear in things printed by Dexter alone. Books bearing his name also contain border ornaments which he and Oulton had used, some of them dating back to Mrs. Allde's *Histrio-Mastix*. And among the initial letters Dexter used are several dating back at least to the partnership days.

In fact, so much of the Oulton and Dexter decorative material appears in the items printed by Dexter alone that there seems good ground for believing that he took over the whole establishment. Possibly Oulton withdrew from the trade entirely, or he may have died. He vanishes, although the old Allde and Oulton-Dexter ornaments remain. Perhaps research in London will reveal what became of him.

The first piece of printing I have been able to identify as printed by Dexter without Oulton is *Mr. Wallers Speech in the House of Commons, On Tuesday the fourth of July, 1643*. John White on 14 July gave his imprimatur to this account of Waller's speech made just before he was expelled from the Commons; how soon after that date the eight-page pamphlet appeared we can only guess, but it was probably very soon.

On 24 June 1643 the Commons had ordered that all news books and pamphlets be entered in the hall book of the Stationers' Company and bear the names of printer and publisher. Since Dexter entered *Waller's Speech* at

SIX GREAT
MATTERS
OF NOTE.

Videlizet,

First, two *Petitions* of the LORDS and
COMMONS to his *Majestie*:
February, 2. 1641.

2. His *Majesties* Answere to the two *Petitions* of the
Lords and *Commons* delivered, as aforesaid.
3. His *Majesties* Consent for the Princesse *Maries*
going to *Holland.*
4. Her *Majesties* Answer to a *Message* of both *Houses.*
5. His *Majesties* *Message* to the *House* of *Commons.*
February, 7. 1641.
6. The humble *Answere* of the Honourable *House* of
Commons to the Kings last *Message,* as aforesaid; in defence
of the Speech lately spoken by Mr. PYMM.

Printed by R. O. and G. D. for F. Coules.

Title; Six Great Matters of Note

ANOTHER
DECLARATION
FROM BOTH
HOUSES
OF
PARLIAMENT:
Sent to His Majesty,
March 23. 1641.

LONDON,
Printed by R. *Oulton* & G. *Dexter.* 1641.

Title; Another Declaration from Parliament

Stationers' Hall on 14 July, the date of the imprimatur, and because it bears only Dexter's name, it was undoubtedly his own venture.

Three days later Dexter entered at Stationers' Hall *A True Relation of the late fight* (at Roundway Down, 13 July) *between Sr. William Wallers forces and those sent from Oxford, with the manner of Sir William Wallers retreat to Bristoll*, but the pamphlet probably was not issued until after 17 July. A third entry was made by Dexter on 19 July. This title is given in the Stationers' Registers as *A Letter out of Staffordshire concerning the taking of Burton by the Queenes forces*, but since no copy of a pamphlet bearing this title has turned up, to my knowledge, it seems most likely that this is what actually appeared as *Stafford-Shires Misery set forth in a true relation of the barbarous cruelty of the forces raised against the Parliament*, by Captain William Robinson. To this latter title the Thomason Catalogue assigns the date of 20 July.

"Printed by G. D. for John Bull, 1643," reads the imprint in *The Inhumanity of the Kings Prison-Keeper at Oxford*, a 32-page tract which also bears the legend, just above the imprint: "Printed according to Order." Thomason's copy is dated 4 August. It was obviously put out to inflame partisans of the Parliament cause, for its sub-title promises to reveal "the most transcendent cruelties, cheatings, cozenings, and base dishonest dealings of William Smith Provest (*sic*) Marshall General of the Kings Army, against the Parliament Prisoners under his custody... Whereunto is added the unsufferable cruelties, exercised upon the Cirencester men, in their passage to Oxford, and at Oxford, in the Castle and Bride-well when they were taken." The latter account was written by Edmund Chillenden. Despite the order of Commons for entering such material in the Registers, this pamphlet was not entered.

On 11 August, Gregory Dexter entered at Stationers' Hall *A pretious & most divine letter from that famous & renowned Earle of Essex father to ye now Lord Generall, &c.*, but if this title was ever printed I know of no copy surviving.

VIII

PRINTER TO ROGER WILLIAMS

Ears have a way of cropping up, or of being cropped, in this story. The ears currently under consideration were those of William Arnold of Pawtuxet, near the head of Narragansett Bay in Rhode Island. They were in jeopardy because Mr. Arnold had cut out of the Town Evidence, the deed by which the Indians conveyed the lands of Providence Plantations to Roger Williams, all reference to Pawtuxet being a part of that grant. Several of his neighbors began clamoring for the Arnold ears when word of his editing got around.

Mr. Arnold's reasons for this mutilation of the deed were obvious. He disliked the way things were going in Providence and had moved to Pawtuxet, only a few miles away. Once there, he sought to divorce himself and his lands from Providence. By mutilating the deed he detached Pawtuxet from the grant, so far as the record was concerned. Then he induced the local sachem to give *him* a deed to Pawtuxet. And then he subjected himself and his lands to Massachusetts Bay, which accepted him on 8 September 1642. Governor Winthrop, remarking on this development in an entry in his journal, noted that the step was designed "to draw in the rest of those parts, either under ourselves or Plimouth."

Roger Williams could see the danger of this situation as easily as Winthrop could estimate its possibilities. Furthermore, the settlements on the Island of Rhode Island, at the mouth of Narragansett Bay, were equally aware of the threat. Hence, eleven days after Pawtuxet had been taken under the wing of Massachusetts the Island men voted to look into the possibility of getting an English patent for Rhode Island "and the lands adjacent."

The following Spring Roger Williams set out to get this patent, taking ship for England at New Amsterdam, his banishment having prevented him from using the port of Boston. During the long days at sea Williams jotted down a mass of notes on the Indian language. These became eventually *A Key into the Language of America: or, An help to the Language of the Natives in that part of America, called New-England*. A more important book, both for its entirely unintended but nonetheless far-reaching effects upon the future of Rhode Island and for its primacy as the first printed work in English devoted exclusively to the Indians and their language, would be hard to imagine.

"I drew the Materialls in a rude lumpe at Sea," writes Williams, in the preface to the reader, "as a private helpe to my owne memory, that I might not by my present absence lightly lose what I had so dearely bought in some few yeares hardship, and charges among the Barbarians; yet being reminded by some, what pitie it were to bury those Materialls in my Grave at land or Sea; and withall, remembring how oft I have been importun'd by worthy friends, of all sorts to afford them some helps this way.

"I resolved (by the assistance of the most High) to cast those Materialls into this Key, pleasant and profitable for All, but specially for my friends residing in those parts."

When Williams reached London the Parliamentary forces were sore beset. The King's armies had been winning notable victories in the west, such as that which Dexter's pamphlet on the battle at Roundway Down had described, and the revolutionary leaders were too busy to discuss such minor matters as patents for colonies on the other side of the ocean. With his friend Sir Henry Vane in Scotland, dickering for aid from that quarter, Roger Williams was delayed in applying for a patent. While he waited for Vane's return he undoubtedly took the opportunity to whip his notes on the Indian language into a book.

What inspired him to take the manuscript to Dexter is something in which one guess is as good as another. Some writers have advanced the theory that John Milton was the means of their meeting. Certainly Milton's connection with this press has been established; in 1641 it had printed at least two of his works and he doubtless would have kept it in mind during the time it was printing pro-Parliament tracts. But whether Milton brought Williams and Dexter together, or whether Williams and Milton met through the printer must remain unanswered questions.

43

Milton and Williams were on friendly terms during Williams' second visit to England, in 1651, and their sharing the same printer in the previous decade may have been the basis of their friendship. On the other hand, there is really no more reason to believe that Milton introduced Williams to Dexter than that any one of several other Parliamentary party leaders might have done so.

I prefer to think that it was because of the position which Dexter held as a printer of New England theological books and pamphlets that Williams went to him. He would have been likely to look for the man who had printed for the men he had known at Boston—with whom, incidentally, Williams always maintained friendly personal relations despite fundamental differences on religious questions. Possibly Williams and Dexter met through Baptist circles, for Williams had paused briefly within the Baptist fold in his slow evolution toward Seekerism, and tradition, via Morgan Edwards, has it that Dexter was a Baptist preacher in London.

Whatever the means by which they met, meet they did, and the result was not only the printing of the *Key* by Dexter but also the formation of a friendship which was to endure for 40 years, as long as Roger Williams lived. This friendship may have had a chance to ripen during visits by the author to Dexter's shop to see how the printing was going. Lawrence C. Wroth once examined five copies of the *Key*, using four typographical errors in three pages as criteria. He came to the conclusion that they "suggest nothing except that Gregory Dexter was sometimes careless in his printing and that somebody, maybe Roger Williams himself, was standing by as the sheets were being printed and insisting upon the press being stopped and corrections made in the forms."[1] Wroth was unable to establish any priority of issue, and said:

"So far as established to the contrary by the existence of these variations we may say that the whole edition of copies made up of correct or of incorrect sheets, or of correct and incorrect sheets mingled, was issued simultaneously."

[1] Wroth, "Variations in Five Copies of Roger Williams' *Key into the Language of America*," in *R. I. H. S. Collections*, XXIX, 120-121.

One of the errors suggests the presence of Williams at the shop, for it is a mistake in the catchword "Sepûo?"— a mistake which might have been allowed to pass by anyone except the author. In one copy this Indian word was printed "8epûo?" but it is given correctly in the other copies I have examined.

The other errors were not of the same sort but seem rather to have been caused by dropped letters or by type being lifted from the forme by sticky ink-balls.[1]

The political effects of the *Key* were far-reaching, as I have said. Quite evidently it made an impression on the Puritan leaders of Parliament when it appeared in the bookstalls in September, 1643,[2] and there is a hint in the Parliamentary Patent which was granted the following March that the Earl of Warwick and his fellow commissioners had found in it concrete evidence of an effort "to make a nearer neighbourhood and Society with the great Body of the Narragansetts, which may in Time by the blessing of God upon their Endeavours, lay a sure Foundation of Happiness to all America."[3] The extent to which the officials were impressed by the book is reflected in the letter they gave Williams to insure his safe passage through the Massachusetts on his way back to Providence. That letter, recorded by Winthrop in his journal under date of 17 September 1644, specifically mentions Williams' "great

---

[1] The variations noted by Wroth are as follows:

Copy	Page 12 Line 20	Page 21 Catch-word	Page 92 Catch-word	Page 92 Line 18
JCB-a	Is the water coo	Chap	8epûo?	Rivelet
JCB-b	Is the wa t er coo	Cha	Sepûo?	Rivulet
JCB-c	Is the water coole?	Chap	Sepûo?	Rivulet
McGregor	Is the water coo	Chap	Sepûo?	Rivulet
RIHS	Is the wa t er coo	Chap	Sepûo?	Rivulet

Another copy in the Rhode Island Historical Society has the page 12 phrase:
Is the water co o le
A copy in the John Hay Library, Brown University, shows this phrase:
Is the w a t er coo
In both these copies the other errors have been corrected.

[2] Thomason dated his copy 7 September 1643.

[3] *R. I. Col. Recs.*, I, 144.

45

industry and travail in his printed Indian labours in your parts, the like whereof we have not seen extant from any part of America, and in which respect it hath pleased both houses of parliament freely to grant unto him and friends with him a free and absolute charter of civil government for those parts of his abode...."

Thus did this little book—so far as I know it was the only octavo volume printed by Dexter—affect history.

On 31 May 1643 the Rev. Andrew Perne, minister at Wilby in Northamptonshire, preached a sermon before the Commons gathered in St. Margaret's Church on the occasion of a public fast. The clerk of the House gave Perne the right to authorize someone to print the sermon, and Perne chose Stephen Bowtell. Bowtell entered the copy at Stationers' Hall on 13 September 1643, "by Order of the House of Commons." This is probably the approximate date when the book appeared, a slight affair of 38 pages, printed by Dexter for Bowtell, and entitled *Gospell Courage, Or Christian Resolution for God, and his Truth.*

We are able to date with accuracy the next product of Dexter's press. It is *The Answer Of The Generall Assembly In Scotland, To The Letter of some of their Reverend Brethren of the Ministry In England, Sent by Mr. Marshall, and Mr. Nye to the said Assembly.* This is a small pamphlet, of only six pages, and was "Ordered to bee Printed." The imprint informs us that it was "Printed by G. Dexter, for Henry Overton. Anno 1643. Sep. 16."

On 29 September 1643 Gregory Dexter entered a title at Stationers' Hall: "A Letter from Hull concerning the present state of that towne dated the 19th of Sept. 1643." Here there is a discrepancy between the entered title and that of the published book, as given in the Thomason Catalogue, which is: *A True Relation from Hull of the present state it is in, in a letter to a Citizen in London.* The Thomason Catalogue ascribes the work to Thomas May and gives it the date of 19 September, using the date of the letter. There seems to be some ground for belief that Dexter entered the copy rather than the finished book, especially since it was entered under his name rather than that of John Bull, for whom it was printed.

Another case of a similar sort is that of *A True and Exact Relation of the Condition of Ireland since the Cessation; a letter from Dublin, 21 Oct.* This is the title as given in the Thomason Catalogue. The pamphlet was printed by Dexter for Henry Overton, and Overton entered it on 16 November as "A true & exact Relacõn of the instant estate of Ireland, &c."

In these cases it is impossible to state with certainty just what did happen. The discrepancy in titles may be due to the scribe's careless way of extracting a "short title." It may be due to entry of manuscript copy rather than printed book. Or it may be due to the Thomason Catalogue's method of extracting a short title, although this last possibility seems extremely remote.

At some time during 1643, Dexter—or it may have been Oulton and Dexter—printed the second edition of John Cotton's *The Doctrine Of The Church, To which are committed the Keys of the Kingdome of Heaven.* This was done for Benjamin Allen and Samuel Satterthwaite, "to be sold in Popes Head Alley and Budge-Row."[1] One reason for the second edition, which indirectly would seem to rule Dexter's shop out of having printed the first edition, is thus stated on the title-page:

"Second Edition: Printed according to a more exact Copy; the Marginall proofes in the former Edition misplaced, being herein placed more directly; and many other faults both in the Line and Margent, are here corrected: And some few proofes and words are added in the Margent, for the better preventing or satisfying of some doubts in some Controversial Points."

This piece was only two sheets folded in quarto but its boasts about the accuracy of the marginal printing show that Dexter's shop professed skill in this respect. *The Doctrine of the Church* bears no printer's name but it contains a head-piece, two types of border ornaments, and an initial *W* to show that it was Dexter's work.

Ostensibly, no more books came from Dexter's press in 1643. Actually, three more tracts, all dated 1644 on their

[1] The latter address may refer to Satterthwaite's shop, although Plomer, in his *Dictionary*, has him at the sign of the Sun, on Garlick Hill, from 1642 to 1649.

title-pages, appeared before 25 March, the beginning of the new year.

The first of these was *Mr. Cottons Letter Lately Printed, Examined And Answered: By Roger Williams of Providence in New-England.*

Some time in 1643 there had been printed for Benjamin Allen *A Letter of Mr. John Cottons Teacher of the Church in Boston, in New-England, to Mr. Williams a Preacher there.* Cotton later contended that this was a private letter, never intended for publication and "how it came to be put in print, I cannot imagine. Sure I am it was without my privitie....There be who thinke it was published by Mr. Williams himselfe, or by some of his friends, who had the Copie from him. Which latter might be the more probable because himselfe denieth the publishing of it...."[1]

However the letter may have happened to get into print Roger Williams quickly seized the opportunity to answer it. Nor was he likely to ignore the effect upon the Puritan leaders of Parliament of an answer to a tract in which Cotton had publicly defended the Boston position that those who "doe not see, nor expressely bewaile the pollutions [i. e., the hated corruptions introduced by the Prelatists] in Church-fellowship, ministery, worship, Government" should not necessarily be barred from church membership.

The result was a 52-page book, *Mr. Cottons Letter Examined,* a copy of which was acquired by Thomason, according to his hand-written date, on 5 February 1643/4. The book was dated forward in the imprint, as was then the practice among printers issuing works near the end of the year.

Dexter's name does not appear on this work; the imprint reads only: "London, | Imprinted in the yeere 1644." But the decoration gives us a clue to the printer. The title-page device consists of eight crowned ornaments, four right-side up and four upside down, within a box of tiny *fleurs de lys.* Here we have this special use of the crowned ornaments which I have noted before. Other border orna-

---

[1] John Cotton, *A Reply To Mr. Williams his Examination; And Answer of the Letters sent to him by John Cotton,* (Narr. Club Pubs., II, 9).

Text; A True Copie of the Masterpiece of . . . . Petitions

A COPPY

OF

A LETTER

of Mr. COTTON of

Boston, in *New* ENGLAND, sent
in answer of certaine Objections
made against their Discipline
and Orders there, directed
to a FRIEND.

VVith the *Questions* propounded to
such as are admitted to the *Church-
fllowship*, and the COVENANT
it SELFE.

Printed in the yeare 1641.

14

Title; A Coppy of a Letter of Mr. Cotton

ments are those known to have been used by Dexter, while the book contains none not used by him before. Lastly, on p. 1 there is a factotum initial which appeared two weeks later in another anonymously printed book by Williams— in which latter book, however, there is an old Allde head-piece as additional proof that Dexter printed it.

The book to which I have just referred is *Queries Of Highest Consideration*. Williams does not appear as the author of this but the fact that he wrote it has been so clearly established that we need not bother ourselves with the proof here. This is a book of considerable importance in the history of the religious controversies which then raged in Revolutionary England. Cotton, in his preface to the *Reply*, mentioned above, places this book third in the series of three written by Williams about this time: *Mr. Cottons Letter Examined*, *The Bloudy Tenent*, and *Queries of Highest Consideration*. But in doing so he probably sought only to assist in the construction of a literary conceit, for he held the first to be an attack on himself, and the second an attack on all the New England churches.

"And then," writes Cotton, "as if New England were but an handful, from thence to rise up against the choicest ornaments of two populous nations, England and Scotland, the reverend Assembly of Divines, together with the reverend Brethren of the Apology, and above them all to address himself, according to his high thoughts, to propound Queries of high Concernment, as he (Williams) calleth them, to the High and Honorable Court of Parliament."

Thomas Goodwin, Philip Nye, William Bridge, Jeremiah Burroughs, and Sidrach Simpson, the Five Dissenting Brethren who were the leaders of the 12 Independents in the Westminster Assembly of Divines, had published in January, 1643/4, *An Apologetical Narration*, in which they sought to determine what degree of compulsion would be required by the new national church based on Presbyterianism. And the Scottish commissioners had presented their apologies in answer.

It was into this situation that Williams plunged with the *Queries of Highest Consideration*, pointing out to both sides and to Parliament that "it shall never be your honor to this or future ages, to be confined to the patterns of either French, Dutch, Scotch or New-English Churches. We humbly conceive some higher acts concerning religion attends and becomes your consultations."

A later writer spoke of this book as an "anonymous pamphlet by some Brownist," meaning an advocate of complete divorcement of the churches one from the other in their own rule and all from the State. It was certainly, in its argument, against government coercion in religious concernments, and hence a foreshadowing of an even more important book to come—*The Bloudy Tenent.*

There is nothing surprising in the fact that the *Queries* was printed anonymously, even as it was written anonymously. But we find, as the headpiece to the preface, one of Edward Allde's old ornaments which had appeared in many Oulton and Dexter works. In this case it was hastily thrust into the forme and hence is upside down. Once more the four crowned ornaments are to be found forming the decorative device on the title-page, and the block initial *I* is that which graced the first page of Pym's *A Speech Delivered At A Conference with the Lords* back in January, 1641/2. These would seem sufficient evidence for naming Gregory Dexter as the printer of the twenty historic pages.

The third anonymously printed book which I assign to the 1643 output of Dexter's press is *A Modest & Brotherly Answer to Mr. Charles Herle his book, against the Independency of Churches...*, by Richard Mather of Dorchester and William Tompson of Braintree, two doughty divines of Massachusetts Bay. Henry Overton, for whom it was printed, entered the title in the Registers on 27 February 1643/4. George Thomason dated his copy on 15 March.

Here again we must rely on the ornamentation to identify the printer. The title-page border is composed of those fleurons which Oulton and Dexter used in the same way on *A True Copie of the Petition of the Gentlewomen and Tradesmens-wives* in 1641 and on *The Petitions of Northampton-Shire And Oxford-Shire* in 1642, and which Dexter alone used to form a headpiece for his *Key* in 1643. In and of themselves these and other border ornaments would hardly be sufficient identification, but when we find the same battered

little block initial *T* on leaf A2 as we did on p. 1 of the *Key*
the argument seems to be ended.

Morgan Edwards preserved a tradition about Gregory
Dexter's removal from London to Providence. He wrote
that Dexter is said "to have been obliged to fly for printing
a piece that was offensive to the then reigning power."

The reigning power in London in 1644 was the Presbyterian party, and in the House of Commons on 9 August
1644 the party ordered a book entitled *The Bloudy Tenent*
to be burned by the public hangman. Years later, in 1671,
Roger Williams wrote to John Cotton, Jr., at Plymouth,
that "'Tis true, my first book, the 'Bloody Tenent,' was
burnt by the Presbyterian party (then prevailing)."

Now the question is: Was the book for printing which
Dexter was forced to flee and *The Bloudy Tenent*[1] which
was burned one and the same?

In my opinion the answer is Yes, and that therefore,
now, after 300 years, we must recognize Gregory Dexter
as the printer of this book, one of the landmarks in Anglo-
Saxon thought and possibly the most important book by
an American prior to the Revolutionary War.[2]

My reasons for claiming that Dexter was the printer are
several. They fall into two classes. First, there are the general, unspecific reasons. Up to the publication of *The
Bloudy Tenent*, at least, all of Roger Williams' printing,
according to my reasoning, had been done by Dexter.
Daring as the contents of *The Bloudy Tenent* may have
seemed at the time, and as they proved to be, there is no
reason for believing that Dexter, having followed Williams
thus far, would have suddenly balked at this job.

Thomason acquired his copy of the book on 15 July,
and the order to burn was given on 9 August. We know
that Roger Williams' suit in chancery, details of which

[1] Here, and elsewhere, when I am discussing Williams' book in general
terms I use the title by which he referred to it, rather than shift back and
forth between *Tenent* and *Tenet* when there is no special need for the
distinction.

[2] For a critical examination of the importance of *The Bloudy Tenent*,
even within the era in which it appeared, see James Ernst, "Roger
Williams and the English Revolution," *R. I. H. S. Collections*, (1931),
XXIV, 1-58 and 118-128.

need not be given here, did not reach the decision stage until 21 June, and therefore Williams undoubtedly did not sail for America before that date.

Now we must retrace our steps a bit, to put our time-table in order. There are two editions of *The Bloudy Tenent*. The type was entirely re-set for the second edition, although there were no significant textual changes and there was apparently an effort to duplicate the typography of the first edition except in the lay-out of the title-page. For years the title of the first edition was thought to be *The Bloudy Tenent*, because that edition contained a sheet of errata. More recently, however, scholarly opinion has settled upon the title which was printed as *The Bloudy Tenet* as that of the first edition.[1]

Just who printed the second edition I am not sure; I am confident, however, that Dexter printed *The Bloudy Tenet*. If we assume that he did, we must come to the conclusion that the edition was sold out or confiscated or destroyed before 15 July, for that is the date on which Thomason apparently acquired his second edition. If *The Bloudy Tenet* had appeared in June, or even earlier, it would have given Dexter time to sense the anger of the ruling powers and to join Williams for the voyage to America, where Williams arrived on or after 17 September.

On the other hand, if Williams sailed without Dexter, late in June or early in July, Dexter may have stayed in London long enough to learn of the Parliamentary order before lighting out for America. In the latter case he may have been the printer of *The Bloudy Tenent*, that is, the second edition.

Thus far I have asked the reader to accept my hypothesis somewhat on faith, plus tradition and generalized reasoning. A close examination of the physical aspects of

[1] Of 23 errors listed in the errata, 14 are correct in the *Tenet* edition, but nine are common to both editions. The assumption is that errors already in the *Tenet* edition were added to in the *Tenent* edition, and that if the *Tenet* were the second edition it would hardly be likely for some of the errors listed in the errata to be corrected and others not.

For a discussion of the problem, see the entries in Sabin: Nos. 104331 and 104332.

The Bloudy Tenet gives us something more concrete on which to base a decision.

The Bloudy Tenet was obviously intended to be an anonymous book; it lacks the names of author and printer and publisher and even the place of publication. It contains not a single printer's device, decorative headpiece, or block initial. Its only embellishment is eight fleurons grouped to make a spot of decoration on the title-page. These are the same type of fleurons which bordered *A Modest & Brotherly Answer to Herle* and which were used to form a headpiece over the caption title in the *Key*.

The roman type of the pages of matter preceding the "To The High Court of Parliament" is the type which appears in the first line of the caption heading on p. 1 of the *Key*. The italic type of the *Tenet* text is the italic used in the poetic "observations" in the *Key*. For example, compare the way in which the capital *W* rests far below the ascender of the lower case *h* whenever the two appear together. The spelling "yeere," which was not a typical Williams spelling, is used with great frequency throughout the *Key* and appears in the imprint of the *Tenet*, as it also does in the imprint of *Mr. Cottons Letter Examined*.

The typographical style of the title-page of the *Tenet*, what we would call today the lay-out or the design, has the "feel" of a Dexter printing job. This is not something which can be dissected. Taken apart, the types mean nothing except that every one of them can be found in some other work by the same printer. But their total effect —the way in which swash italic capitals are used, the pattern of the italicizing, and the way in which the lines are stepped down in size—these all convey to me the "feel" of Dexter's work.

Of less importance perhaps but still significant is the fact that the printer of both the *Key* and the *Tenet* abbreviated Chapter to Chap. The type used in Williams' signature at the end of the "To the Reader" in the *Key* is the same as is used in the word "Conference" in the caption heading on p. 15 of the *Tenet;* it was either cast on a broad-shouldered body or else Dexter ordinarily opened it up with spaces. The italic type in *Language* on the title-page of the *Key* is the same as that in *Newgate* on p. 1 of the *Tenet*, as may be seen by comparing the lower case *g* in each instance.

There are other comparisons of this same sort which can be made, proving the identities of the types. But perhaps the strongest evidence to be drawn from the types themselves is found in the roman small capitals used to set Roger Williams' name on the title-page of the *Key* and to set CHAP in the various chapter headings of the *Tenet*. Here is a mixed font; it contains letters of two sizes, the larger being 3 mm. in height and the smaller 2-1/2 mm.

Of course Gregory Dexter was not the only printer in London in 1644 who had a mixed font in his cases. But the fact that the same font is mixed in both the *Key* and the *Tenet* seems to be at least the one additional grain of evidence needed to tip the scales and establish Gregory Dexter as the printer of *The Bloudy Tenet*.

The last thing we have to add about Dexter's London career comes to us from tradition, via Isaiah Thomas. He wrote that Dexter printed a 1644 almanac for Providence Plantations in New England. A likely possibility, but unfortunately no copy has ever turned up since Thomas' statement became public knowledge.

IX

INTO THE WILDERNESS

UNDER THE date of 17 September 1644, Governor John Winthrop of Massachusetts Bay wrote in his journal that "here arrived also Mr. Roger Williams of Providence, and with him two or three families."

Gregory Dexter may have been in this party, bound for Rhode Island; possibly he did not arrive until later. But, despite certain claims that he was in Providence before the Autumn of 1644, I think it can be shown conclusively that this was not the case.

The "evidence" that Gregory Dexter was in Providence earlier than this is confined to two documents, both of which have been held to bear dates prior to 1644. However, it was not until after John Russell Bartlett began editing the printed edition of *Rhode Island Colonial Records* in 1856 that historians started to say that Dexter was in Providence before 1643 or 1644.

Morgan Edwards wrote that Dexter "came to Providence in 1643." Isaiah Thomas wrote that soon after printing Williams' *Key* (i.e., 1643) and the first almanac for Providence Plantations, "Dexter quitted printing, left his native country, and joined Williams in Providence, where he became a distinguished character in the colony." Jonathan Dexter, Gregory's great-great-grandson, had written in his manuscript genealogy in 1819 that Dexter "Came to Providence in 1643..." In fact, no writer before Bartlett's time ever placed Dexter in Providence before 1643, so far as I can discover, and several careful historians, working after Bartlett, saw that what seemed to be evidence of an earlier arrival was not actually proof of that theory. But, since many have assumed Bartlett's evidence to be infallible and since it was given wide circulation in Austin's *Genealogical Dictionary of Rhode Island*, it must be examined here for its true worth.

On p. 24 of Volume I of *Rhode Island Colonial Records* there is a lengthy footnote referring to the granting of home-lots and six-acre lots to 54 persons, early settlers of Providence. Although the marginal date on this page of the book is 1638, Bartlett states that this note is based on a document preserved in the Providence City Clerk's office, entitled "A revised list (saving corrections with additions) of lands and meadows as they were originally lotted from the beginning of the plantation...unto the (then) inhabitants of the said plantation anno 16—."

Note that Bartlett did not give this date as anything but 16—. The list seems to have been lost but Charles W. Hopkins had examined it and made a verbatim transcription of it in preparing his *The Home Lots of the Early Settlers of the Providence Plantations* (Providence, 1886), and he says that it was dated 1660 in another place and was written by Roger Williams. This date, plus the fact that the list contains names of several persons known to have arrived

GREGORY DEXTER

in Providence after 1640, makes the list worthless as proof
that Dexter was in Providence as early as 1638.[1]

The second document which might lead one to believe
that Dexter was in Providence before 1643 or 1644 was the
so-called "Combination of 1640," which Dexter signed.
This was an agreement for the primitive government of
the infant town. Unfortunately, again the original document has been lost. Bartlett neglected to mention that fact
when he printed the text and the appended signatures in
Rhode Island Colonial Records, I, 27. The surviving text, which
Bartlett used, is actually a later copy, made by Thomas
Olney, Jr., the Providence town clerk, on 28 March 1662.[2]

Careful examination of this document, such as that to
which it was subjected by Howard M. Chapin in his
Documentary History of Rhode Island, I, 110-120, shows that
some of the residents of the town on 5 July 1640, the date of
the agreement, did not sign it, but that it *was* signed by
persons who did *not* arrive in Providence until after that
date. It seems, therefore, that this was an "open" agreement, to which persons affixed their signatures whenever
they agreed to abide by its terms. In this light we can see
that its date does not necessarily prove that Gregory Dexter
was here when it was first drawn up.

That he came later is shown, for one thing, by the position of his home-lot. This was at the northern extremity
of the row of lots, alongside a lane to which he shortly gave
his name and which has since become Olney Street. The
home-lot of Robert Williams, Roger's brother, who was
probably also a member of the party which arrived in
Boston in September, 1644, was at the extreme southern end
of the row. Since the town grew north and south along one
highway, at first known as the Towne Street and now
named North and South Main streets, expanding from a

[1] My own opinion is that here Bartlett was not at fault. Careless
interpretation of his material seems to have been more to blame. That
and Austin's inclusion of the material as fact in his *Genealogical Dictionary*.

[2] It is Providence Town Paper #02, now in the Providence City Hall.
It is printed in *Prov. Recs.*, XV, 2-5. It is of interest to note that this Olney
copy shows signs of an attempt at facsimile. The names of Dexter and
Robert Williams are written up and down, in the left margin although
there was room for them elsewhere.

56

To the READER.

His Veſſell once hath lanc'd into the Maine
But being landed, muſt to Sea againe,
Her decks repair'd, and every place beſide
Shee'l venture once more on the falling Tyde
Fraught with more Reliques, then ſhe was before
Such as Romes Conclave long hath kept in ſtore
Ship-ſplitting Rocks, with fearce tempeſtious wind
Shee dreads not (READER) if thou be'ſt but kind
If Boreas ſtorme, and all the Winds beſide,
Thy kind acceptance will allay their pride,
be not prejudicate, but if thine eye
Pry out their faults, be pleaſ'd to paſſe them by.

Thus then, ſhe ventures, to preſent her Ware,
And bids you welcome to New Lambeth-Fayre.

NEVV

Verso of Title; New Lambeth Fayre

THE
PETITIONS
OF
NORTHAMPTON-SHIRE
AND
OXFORD-SHIRE.

PRESENTED
VNTO THE HIGH COVRT
OF
PARLIAMENT:

LONDON,
Printed by R. *Olton,* and G. *Dexter.* for *Benjamin Allen,* and *John Bull.* MDCXLII.

Title; Northamptonshire and Oxfordshire Petitions

center near the spring opposite the lot of Roger Williams, the positions of Dexter's and Robert Williams' lots would indicate that they were late arrivals.

There is other negative evidence that Dexter was not here before 1644. With the two exceptions noted above, his name appears nowhere in the town records before that year, but in the ensuing years, starting about 1646, his name becomes remarkably prominent. Also, there is the evidence of Roger Williams' deed of 1661, in which he wrote:

"...And besides the First that were admitted, our Towne Recordes declare, that afterwards wee Received Chad Browne, William Feild, Thomas Harris Senior, William Wickenden, Robert Williams, Grigorey Dexter, and others as or Towne Booke declares:..."[1]

Here, then, is the situation:

If we except the two Bartlett documents, one of which is unquestionably not pertinent, while the other is open to serious doubts, there is not a shred of evidence that Dexter arrived in Providence before 1643 or 1644. Before Bartlett printed those documents and, what is even more important, before Austin gave them prominence in his *Genealogical Dictionary of Rhode Island*, no biographer of Dexter ever placed him in Providence before 1643 or 1644.

On the other hand, Dexter's books, especially those anonymously printed pamphlets which I have traced to his press, are evidence that he was in London, pursuing his trade, well into 1644. By 1646 he is one of the most prominent figures in the colony. Is it likely that he would have taken no part in public affairs for either six or eight years and then suddenly blossomed out as a leading citizen? I cannot believe that even the firebrands of King Philip's War were so discriminating in their destruction of town records.

There remains but one other question about an "early" Gregory Dexter in Providence. In his *The Cambridge Press* (Philadelphia, 1945), on p. 73, George Parker Winship advances the hypothesis that Dexter could have had a

---

[1] *Prov. Recs.*, V, 307.

father of the same name residing in Providence before the son arrived in 1644, or later. Winship contends that the man of whom Morgan Edwards wrote was "hipped on religion and an uncomfortable neighbor in settled society," and that Gregory the printer "cannot have been the persistent bore whose character was described to Morgan Edwards."

Edwards wrote:

"Mr. Dexter by all accounts was not only a well-bred man, but remarkably pious. He was never observed to laugh, seldom to smile. So earnest was he in his preaching that he could hardly forbear preaching when he came into a house, or met with a concourse of people out of doors."[1]

Granting that the man of this description was somewhat different from the one described by Roger Williams, in a letter to John Winthrop, Jr.,[2] as possessed of "a very willing heart, (being a sanguine, cheerful man)," there seems to be a good resemblance to the man whose character Williams was analyzing in a letter to John Whipple, Jr., only a month earlier.[3] This letter is, in many ways, the most elaborate analysis of Dexter's character which has come down to us, and consequently the entire pertinent section is quoted:

"...The last night, Shadrach Manton told me that I had spoken bad words of Gregory Dexter, (though Shadrach deals more ingenuously than yourself saying the same thing, for he tells me wherein,) viz.: that I said *he makes a fool of his conscience.*[4] I told him I said so, and I think to our neighbor Dexter himself; for I believe he might as well be moderator or general deputy or general assistant, as go as far as he goes, in many particulars; but what if I or my conscience be a fool, yet it is commendable and admirable in him, that being a man of education, and of a noble calling, and versed in militaries, that *his conscience forced him to be such a child in his own house,*[4] when W. Har. strained for the rate (which I approve of) with such imperious insulting

[1] Edwards, *History*, p. 321.

[2] *Narragansett Club Publications*, VI, 332. The letter is dated at Providence, 19 August 1669.

[3] *Narr. Club Pubs.*, VI, 328. The letter is dated at Providence, 8 July 1669.

[4] Italics are mine.

over his conscience, which all conscientious men will abhor to hear of. However, I commend that man, whether Jew or Turk, or Papist, or whoever, that steers no otherwise than his conscience dares, till his conscience tells him that God gives him a greater latitude.

"For, neighbor, you shall find it rare to meet with men of conscience, men that for fear and love of God dare not lie, nor be drunk, nor be contentious, nor steal, nor be covetous, nor voluptuous, nor ambitious, nor lazy-bodies, nor busy-bodies, nor dare displease God by omitting either service or suffering, though of reproach, imprisonment, banishment and death, because of the fear and love of God...."

X

ALMANACS AT CAMBRIDGE

GREGORY DEXTER seems to have turned his back on his trade as a way of life, once he reached America. It would have been absurd to think of setting up a press in Providence Plantations, considering the miniscule size of the infant colony, its really primitive cultural development in Dexter's time, and the almost universal dependence of the few inhabitants on agriculture and the simplest sort of commerce for an existence. Providence, indeed, had no need for a press until three decades after Dexter was dead.

In the Massachusetts Bay colony, however, things were different. Not only was there a press in that settlement when Dexter arrived in America, but evidently there was also a need for someone to run it if any ambitious printing was to be undertaken.

The Cambridge Press, according to Winship, had lain more or less idle since the printing of the *Bay Psalm Book*. In 1642 and 1643 Harvard Commencement *Theses* were printed, although no copy of the former is known to have survived. In 1642, also, the broadside *Capitall Lawes* was printed at the press, and possibly a book label for Steven Day and a little spelling book. No copy of the first and last of this trio has survived, but there is no reason for assuming that either one of them presented any serious problem for a printer.

Between the *Bay Psalm Book* of 1640 and *A Declaration of Former Passages and Proceedings Betwixt the English and the Narrowgansets*, published on 11 August 1645, nothing of any typographical complexity is known to have come from the Cambridge Press. No one, so far as I know, has ever advanced the theory that Gregory Dexter may have helped to print the seven-page *Narragansett Declaration*, although he was probably less than 50 miles away when the work was in the press. Nor do I intend to advance that theory now.

Although Morgan Edwards wrote that "about the year 1646 he [Dexter] was sent for to Boston, to set in order the printing office there," and thus Dexter might have had a hand in the *Narragansett Declaration*, which was done near enough to this date, the pamphlet bears not the slightest trace of his work. Certainly he was not responsible for the composition, if we presume that he set the type for any of the other books printed by him. The first glance at the text matter of the *Narragansett Declaration* reveals a typographical peculiarity: the compositor left considerable space after many of his commas, apparently as an easy way of making his lines justify. In all the Gregory Dexter imprints I have examined I have never seen one which showed this peculiar practice.

This business of spacing widely after commas is, in one sense, a sign that Dexter had not yet come to the assistance of the press, for, as a London trade printer, he knew other ways to make lines justify and undoubtedly he would have imparted his knowledge to the Cambridge compositor. There is a much better case for Dexter's hand being in the 1651 Psalm Book.

If Dexter did not help out with the *Narragansett Declaration*, there is nonetheless strong evidence that he had a hand in producing the next known output of the Cambridge Press: an almanac for 1646.

Although one almanac is recorded as having been produced by the press prior to the appearance of the *Bay Psalm Book*, Winship, in *The Cambridge Press*, has argued on the basis of the paper consumption allotted to theses and almanacs that most likely no almanacs appeared before 1646, with the single exception already noted.

Edwards, in a continuation of the quotation given earlier, stated that for his services in setting the Cambridge Press in order Dexter "desired no other reward than that one of their almanacs should be sent him every year," and Isaiah Thomas, quoting from the manuscript papers of President Ezra Stiles of Yale, wrote:

"It is said that after Samuel Green began printing at Cambridge, Dexter went there annually, for several years, to assist him in printing an almanac."[1]

The earliest New England almanac which has survived to us is one for the year 1646. This and four others, for the ensuing four years, were sewn together by their original owner. The 1646 almanac, lacking the title-page and the following leaf, is now in the Henry E. Huntington Library. Its damaged condition prevents us from knowing whether Dexter's name appeared on it—a somewhat slim possibility anyway. Frankly, there is nothing about the composition which reminds especially of Dexter, but in such a piece of printing it would hardly be expected, and it is also interesting to note that the typographical style differs somewhat between this first almanac and others of the same group.

On the other hand, there seems to be no serious ground for doubting that Gregory Dexter helped to get it out, especially in view of Morgan Edwards' statement and the supplemental evidence of the Stiles memorandum. But these almanacs, signifying perhaps a few brief returns to a former way of life, are about the only pieces of printing done on this side of the Atlantic which can be even tentatively ascribed to Dexter. Except for them he disappears from printing in America as completely as that George Wapull to whom his fellow-members of the Stationers' Company gave 10 shillings in 1585 "toward his voyage into Norumbegue."[2]

Why, one may ask, if the press at Cambridge needed a skilled printer, and Gregory Dexter was aware of this chance to follow his old trade in a new land, did he fail to transfer his home from Providence to Cambridge?

[1] Thomas, *History of Printing in America* (2nd edition), p. 194.
[2] Arber, *Transcript*, I, 509.

There are several answers. One, of course, was the fact that the press was owned by someone else, and Dexter would have been only its operator rather than its proprietor. Secondly, it is doubtful if the Cambridge Press at the moment was in need of anything more than the brief touch of an expert. It seems hardly likely that there was a good living in it.

But, most important, there was the matter of Dexter's religion. Edwards says he was "both a baptist and a preacher before his arrival," and was received into the Baptist Church at Providence the same year that he arrived. If this statement is accurate we can easily understand why Dexter would not be tempted by Cambridge. Speaking euphemistically, the Bay's attitude toward Baptists was hardly congenial, when it wasn't downright terrifying. As a Baptist, Dexter would have been barred from the privileges of a freeman, to say nothing of standing in danger of more serious difficulties. The Bay offered hardly the intellectual climate which would naturally be sought by a man who had the friends and connections that Dexter had in his London days. A printer of his stripe would have been quick to detect the fact that fleeing from London to Boston resembled somewhat more than remotely the trip from the frying-pan to the fire.

All these circumstances pointed in only one direction: Providence and his old friend Roger Williams. In that community, men of Gregory Dexter's stature and experience were sorely needed. There he could work out his salvation in an atmosphere of religious freedom and political liberty. There he could find something approaching the Utopia for which, ever since apprentice days, he had constantly hazarded at least his ears if not his life.

XI

OPPORTUNITY KNOCKS

ONCE Gregory Dexter had reached Providence Plantations he became, almost immediately, one of the colony's leaders. Roger Williams had brought back with him in September the so-called Patent of 1644, the instrument of government which was to provide the colony with its first real basis for self-rule. Previously the settlement's affairs had been handled by the most elemental sort of government. At first there was nothing but a system of informal and irregular meetings of the heads of households, supplemented, before Dexter's arrival, by a crude arbitration system.

But the Patent granted the inhabitants of Providence, Portsmouth, and Newport "a free and absolute charter of incorporation....Together with full Power and Authority to rule themselves...by such a Form of Civil Government, as by voluntary consent of all, or the greater Part of them, they shall find most suitable to their Estate and Condition." The Patent also gave the towns power to make laws, inflict punishments on those who broke them, and to "place and displace" officials to execute them.

Providence Plantations, when the Patent arrived, was suffering from an acute shortage of men capable of setting up and putting into operation any such government. The Island towns had their share of leaders, for among their inhabitants were men who had been prominent in the government of Massachusetts Bay until the religious squabble over Antinomianism and taxes had caused them to depart in dudgeon. In people like William Coddington, John Coggeshall, William Brenton, Dr. John Clarke, and the Hutchinsons, the Island towns had capable men of experience and, whatever weaknesses they may have revealed in subsequent events, there was no gainsaying that they knew how to lead.

By contrast Providence lacked not only an over-all cohesiveness but also any sizable group with a sense of leadership. The settlement on the Moshassuck had been made by men with but one common aim and that a negative one: to get out from under the religious oppression of Massachusetts. Some of the settlers were scarcely more than boys, and others were widows. Furthermore, though their primary rebellion—the one for which they are most commonly remembered in local history—was against religious domination, it must be kept in mind that at that time rebellion against restraints in religion and rebellion against any governmental restraint whatsoever were often indistinguishable, if not actually identical. William Harris, one of the more rambunctious malcontents, tried to extend the principle of liberty of conscience to mean that he did not have to pay allegiance to any government among men if he could say that to do so violated his conscience.

Such men were more interested in escaping government than they were in setting it up. In addition, the settlement was handicapped by a lack of men of education. Harris is thought by some historians to have been a lawyer's clerk in old England, although Roger Williams says he was a Morris dancer in Kent. However that may be, Harris did not put his peculiar legal talents to use at all during this formative period; he was a forceful leader in the Providence land disputes, but those did not begin in earnest for more than 10 years after Dexter's arrival. Harris, like most of the other capable men, had removed from the town proper by 1644; others had spread into such outlying parts as Pawtuxet or started new settlements at Warwick. The Warwick men had been shattered by a ruthless invasion from Massachusetts, and the Pawtuxet men in William Arnold's faction had subjected themselves in 1642 to the Bay, thus becoming alienated from Providence. The town did number some able men among its inhabitants, however, and these included Thomas Olney, Chad Brown, William Wickenden, (all three, like Dexter, leaders in the Baptist church) and John Throckmorton, Thomas Harris, William Field, and John Lippitt.

But when Robert Williams, Roger's brother, and Gregory Dexter arrived, either with or shortly after the Patent, there was plenty of room for them at the top of the heap, and so great was the need for abilities such as they possessed that they were not long in rising to positions of prominence.

THE
PEASANTS·PRICE
OF
SPIRITVALL LIBERTY.

VVherein is reprefented the *Complexion*
of the *Times*, and *Confiderations*
to Cure it.

In three *Sermons*.

By *Nathaniel Homes*, D. D.

LONDON,
Printed by *R. O.* and *G. D.* for *Benjamin Allen*
in *Popefhead Alley*, 1642.

Title; Peasants Price of Spirituall Liberty

A Modeſt and Cleare

ANSWER
TO
Mr Balls Diſcourſe of
ſet formes of PRAYER.

Set forth in a moſt Seaſonable time, when
this KINGDOME is now in Conſultation about
Matters of that Nature, and ſo many godly
Long after the Reſolution in that Point.

Written by the Reverend and Learned, *John Cotton*,
B. D. and Teacher of the Church of Chriſt at
Boſton in new *England*.

LONDON,
Printed by R. O. and G. D. for *Henry Overton*,
in *Popes head-Alley*, 1642.

Title; Cotton's Answer to Ball

Robert Williams promptly settled at the extreme southern end of the row of houselots which faced westward onto
the Towne Street, now North and South Main Streets,
and Gregory Dexter built his home at the opposite end of
the row, near what is now Olney Street but which was
known for years as Dexter's Lane.

There was something almost symbolic about this geo-
graphical distribution of homes—Roger Williams living
almost at the middle of the row while Brother Robert
buttressed one end and friend Gregory the other. For,
together, but always with Roger Williams as the focal
point, these three men did the main part of the work—so
far as Providence was concerned—of setting up the colony
under Patent government and of maintaining it there
during a period of great trial.[1]

It is interesting, then, to note that these three men and
Thomas Olney were chosen by the town to obtain from
Ousamequin, chief sachem of the Wampanoags, a deed
clearing title to lands between Pawtucket and Louisquisset,
north of Providence, which the townsmen claimed had
been granted them years earlier in the original deed from
the Narragansett sachems and wherein Dexter was to find
in later years his limestone quarry. And is it not proof of
the rapidity with which Dexter's worth was recognized
that he was named to this Indian mission?

The four-man delegation made the trip to Ousamequin's
lodge at Wapewasick, on the mainland opposite Portsmouth, in the summer of 1646. According to a deposition
made by the four agents on 10 September 1646, the deed
was given by the sachem on 9 August but then the Indian
refused to sign, holding out for an unreasonable number of

---

[1] The part played by Robert Williams in getting the government of
Providence on its feet has been neglected by local historians, probably
because most local history is written by genealogists and Robert Williams,
being apparently without issue, was not of interest to genealogists. This
is not the place to go into a lengthy discussion of the case but it is worthy
of note that Robert Williams was one of the two town deputies through
almost all the years that Dexter was town clerk, that he generally sat
with Dexter as one of the six Providence commissioners to the General
Court, and that he often served as moderator of town meetings in this
period.

coats, hoes, knives, axes, and other trading truck, after having received what he originally asked for.[1]

The next task to which the town assigned Gregory Dexter was one of great importance. After more than two years of stalling and bickering a move got under way in the Spring of 1647 to set up a government under the Patent. Ten commissioners were chosen by Providence as delegates to this "constitutional convention." They are named and given instructions from the town in a letter written by Roger Williams on 16 May 1647. Dexter's name leads the list of commissioners; the others were William Wickenden, Thomas Olney, Robert Williams, Richard Waterman, Roger Williams, William Field, John Greene, John Smith, and John Lippitt.

The commissioners were empowered to do their best to bring about "the setling of the Jland in peace and Vnion," thereby ending the squabbling between Newport and Portsmouth, and "to moue, and procure any things, (beside these Jnstructions) that in yor wisdome you conceiue may tend, vnto the Generall peace & Vnion of the Colonye, and our owne perticular Liberties, and privilledges...."

This General Court sat at Portsmouth on 19, 20, and 21 May, and drew up the Code of Laws of 1647 which was to be the operating basis of the colony government in Rhode Island until the Patent was supplanted by the King Charles II Charter of 1663.

The year following, when another General Court was held on 16 May, at Providence, it was ordered that six men from each of the four towns—Warwick had entered the colony union—should be chosen, "in whom the General Court shall continue." Those chosen for Providence were Thomas Olney, Thomas Harris, William Wickenden, Hugh Bewitt, Robert Williams, and Gregory Dexter, the

---

[1] There may be a discrepancy in the dates here; the deposition seems to have been made the day after the date of the deed. The deed and deposition are in *R. I. Col. Recs.*, I, 33-34. The original of the deposition, in Roger Williams' handwriting, is in the collection of W. Easton Louttit, Jr., of Providence. Of interest is the fact that the grantees named in the deed are Dexter and Roger Williams, and the other inhabitants of Providence. This is, therefore, the first indisputable date of Gregory Dexter's being settled at Providence.

six men who were to be the political leaders of Providence for the next five years.

Dexter had become town clerk of Providence as early as 24 August 1648, when he held three persons under bonds for trial, signing himself "Gregory Dexter Town-Clerk."[1] There is no record of his election, and hence we do not know how long he had been holding the office. The first record of Dexter's election to this office is in 1651, but it appears from ample evidence, such as signatures similar to the one above, that he was holding the office on 19 June 1649, on 24 July 1650, and on 15 November 1651.[2]

Dexter held the town clerk's office for several years, relinquishing it only in 1655, when his successor was John Sayles, Roger Williams' son-in-law. Although the election records for every year are not extant, it can be shown that Dexter was town clerk of Providence from 1648 to 1655.

He served as an arbitrator in a case decided in December 1648 under the town's quaint legal system, and in the same year he testified to seeing his good friend and fellow official, Robert Williams, drunk.[3]

On 3 November 1648 he bought land of Joshua Windsor, it being a share of meadow on the west side of the Moshassuck River. The next year he did two little chores for the town. On 9 May 1649, he and Hugh Bewitt were sent to inquire of Benedict Arnold whether "the Planting Field at Pawtugug" (Pawtucket?) was his, and with Robert Williams, Thomas Harris, and Bewitt he served on a committee of townsmen to wait upon John Smith's widow and once more "assay to make agreements" about the operation of the town's one grist mill. He also served on the "grand inquest" in 1649. At the General Assembly for Elections at Newport in 1650 Gregory Dexter was again a commissioner from Providence. Serving with him were Richard

---

[1] *Prov. Recs.*, XV, 17.

[2] *Prov. Recs.*, XV, 23-25, 31, 47. Staples, in *Annals of the Town of Providence* (Providence, 1843), p. 79, says that 1651 is the first year in which there is any record of a choice of town officers. There is ample evidence, however, that the town had officers besides a clerk at least two years before that date.

[3] *Prov. Recs.*, XV, 21. His testimony was corroborated.

Waterman, Thomas Hopkins, Hugh Bewitt, Arthur Fenner, and Thomas Harris.[1]

The earliest of the Providence tax lists which have been preserved to us is that dated 2 September 1650. In it Dexter was taxed £1, which appears to be the figure for those land-owners who had received only the regular full allotment of home-lot, six-acre lot, and share of meadow. In July he had made a true copy of the so-called Pawtuxet Agreement, signing as town clerk. This was the agreement which set off Pawtuxet as the exclusive property of the original 13 proprietors named in the 1638 deed from Roger Williams. This agreement[2] was to become the basis for the protracted land disputes which wracked the town for nearly a century; it will be discussed in detail later when Dexter's part in those disputes is taken up.

In 1650, too, Dexter and Nicholas Power were named to collect "the goods belonging to the children of Daniel Abbott deceased," including some goats, and to dispose of them for the benefit of the children. This same year the town passed an ordinance requiring registration of births, with the town clerk to get three pence for each one he recorded. The alert responsiveness of the townspeople to such a rule is perhaps best indicated by the fact that Dexter himself did not bother to enter the births of his own children until 27 May 1653, although his oldest son, Stephen, had been born on 1 November 1647, and his second son, James, on 6 May 1650, about the time the order was passed. In all, the births of four children of Gregory Dexter and Abigail, his wife, are recorded.[3] John, the third son, was born 6 November 1652, and Abigail on 27 September 1655.

Of Mrs. Dexter we know very little. Her maiden name is given by several genealogists, all of them apparently using Edwards' material, as Fullerton, or Fuller, but where she came from or when she and Gregory Dexter were married remains a mystery. She survived her husband by at least six years, for she was living as late as 1706.

[1] *Prov. Recs.*, II, 9, 41, 43, 49; XV, 25; Staples, *Annals*, p. 76.
[2] *Prov. Recs.*, XV, 33, 31.
[3] *Prov. Recs.*, II, 49; I, 7.

One of Dexter's attributes of value to the town was his fluency as a writer. Not only was he able to perform the physical task of a penman, which was a sufficiently rare accomplishment in Providence at that time, but he also was able to compose the letters. On 2 September 1650 he was directed to write to Massachusetts in an attempt to settle the claims of creditors against the deceased Edward Cope. At the same meeting he became, in a sense, town treasurer, for Hugh Bewitt was ordered to serve notice on property owners of their share in a rate and, when he received any payment, to turn it over to Dexter, "who is appointed to receive it for the Townes use."[1] It is of interest to note that Robert Williams was town moderator at these meetings in 1650; he and Thomas Harris had been chosen town deputies at an earlier election, the specific date of which has been torn from the record, and these two, with Dexter, Olney, and Bewitt, were pretty much running town affairs. Dexter and Olney were chosen by the town on 28 October 1650 to negotiate some sort of agreement with the Widow Smith about a highway near her mill and about the mill itself. It seems that the mill problem was still unsettled.[2]

XII

LEFT IN CHARGE

In August, 1651, William Coddington brought off a *coup d'état* which threw the colony into complete confusion. The Island's power-seeking leader had returned from England that month with a Parliamentary commission which made him virtually ruler for life of the Island of Aquidneck and its two towns. This superseded the Williams Patent of 1644 and deprived the colony of Providence Plantations of its two richest components: Portsmouth and Newport. Already weakened on the mainland by the defection of Arnold's faction at Pawtuxet, which had subjected to

---

[1] *Prov. Recs.*, II, 51. This is not the first record of a town treasurer; Thomas Olney served as such in 1638.

[2] *Prov. Recs.*, II, 52.

Massachusetts, and by a similar step on the part of the Cowesett sachem, Pomham, and by the Massachusetts threats against Warwick, Providence faced a bleak future indeed.

Promptly a move was launched to send Roger Williams to London to seek an overthrow of the Coddington commission, and Coddington's opponents on the Island, acting independently, dispatched Dr. John Clarke, squired by William Dyer, on a similar mission. When Williams departed, to take ship at Boston in November, leadership in the town's affairs, and in those of the shattered colony government, devolved either naturally or by plan upon Robert Williams, Gregory Dexter, Thomas Olney, Thomas Harris, and such supporters as they could muster. Olney eventually broke with the others, probably because of either land disputes or a Baptist church schism, but for a time he helped to run the town affairs. At the town election in 1651, for instance, Olney was moderator; he and Robert Williams were chosen town deputies; Thomas Harris was made town treasurer; and Gregory Dexter once more was elected town clerk.

When the crisis caused by Coddington occurred, an emergency meeting of representatives from the two mainland towns was held on 23 October 1651 and Samuell Gorton was chosen president of the colony. It was ordered that six men from each town be chosen to meet at Providence on 4 November 1651 "and there consult and determine, of what may make for the publique good of the Colonie." Representing Providence at this November session were Robert Williams, Thomas Harris, Hugh Bewitt, William Wickenden, Thomas Olney, and Gregory Dexter. These men and the six from Warwick promptly formulated a statement declaring their two towns "to stand inbodyyed and incorporated as before, by virtue of our charter," and then called for an election the following May at Warwick. The Providence delegates to this May meeting were "Mr. Robert" Williams, "Mr. Gregorie" Dexter, Richard Waterman, Thomas Harris, William Wickenden, and Hugh Bewitt. Thomas Olney was elected general assistant for Providence, and John Smith of Warwick supplanted

Gorton, who was sick and tired of the office and declared that the best qualification to hold a public position was an ability to take abuse. Gorton stepped down from president to assistant for Warwick. Providence, in choosing its delegates to this Court of Election, had nominated Robert Williams for president, Olney and Arthur Fenner for assistant, Hugh Bewitt for general sergeant, and Gregory Dexter for general recorder.

Of these, only Olney and Bewitt were elected.

This succeeded in setting up, however weakly, the colony government. Turning to Dexter's part in town affairs we discover that he sold land to the son of John Smith, the deceased miller, and got permission from the town to exchange one six-acre meadow for another. As town clerk he was called upon to answer a letter from Joshua Verin, who had left Providence years earlier after having been disfranchised for restraining his wife in her choice of religious services. Verin had written the town asking to be sustained in his right to his property in Providence. Dexter, ordered on 27 April 1651 to send him a reply, promptly did so in a terse note in which the town stated that "if yu shall come unto or Court, & Prove yr right, they will doe yu Justice."

In August, 1651, William Cotton, a Boston butcher, was arrested on complaint of William Field of Providence, in a suit in the Providence court to recover a £10 debt. Gregory Dexter became attorney for Cotton, his first and only venture as a lawyer, so far as I can learn. He lost the case, a verdict being returned on 6 October giving Field his requested £10 plus damages of £3/15/00 and costs. There was a request for an appeal but Dexter advised his client it was too late to take such a step. Benedict Arnold, who had gone bail for Cotton, sought an answer to the request for an appeal from Field himself. Apparently he got nowhere with this move. If the colony had seriously considered granting it all hope flew out the window when John Sayles swore that Massachusetts authorities had made threats against the Providence jurisdiction. Sayles swore that Cotton had told him of discussing the case informally with a group of Bay magistrates, some of whom suggested sending a letter to Providence "to know a reason of their proceedings in the said suit: to wch m^r Dudley being Debt; Governour being then present replyed, a Sword if anything." This sealed the doom of Cotton's cause.[1]

XIII

PRESIDENT OF
PROVIDENCE PLANTATIONS

AN IMPORTANT episode in Rhode Island history in which Gregory Dexter played a leading part was the trial of Hugh Bewitt, his political colleague and the colony's general sergeant, on charges of high treason.

In June, 1652, John Smith of Warwick, president of the two-town colony, had shipped some tobacco, peas, and flour to Newfoundland for Christopher Almy, the minor son of William Almy, Portsmouth planter. On board the vessel, the Providence of Pequot, Ralph Parker master, on her return to Providence was a supply of Dutch brandy which, presumably, the Almys had received in exchange for their goods. According to witnesses Smith withheld 55 gallons of the liquor to pay freight charges, but the Almys objected that he was computing the quantity at the price of brandy in Newfoundland whereas they wanted to pay the charges in brandy at the Providence price or in other goods. An impasse ensued, Smith kept the 55 gallons of brandy, and William Almy brought suit against him, with Hugh Bewitt as his attorney.

On 9 November Bewitt committed himself to prosecute charges against Smith or to pay the charges, and forthwith, over the signature of Gregory Dexter as town clerk, a warrant for Smith's arrest was issued to Thomas Wallin, town sergeant.

Almy was in the Providence town court of trials, ready to proceed, on 7 and 8 December, but Robert Williams,

[1] The documents in the Field-Cotton suit are in *Prov. Recs.*, XV, 46, 47, 49, and 84.

INSTRUCTIONS

Agreed upon

By the *LORDS* and *COMMONS*

IN

PARLIAMENT,

FOR

The Deputy *Lieutenants* for the County

of *Lincolne and by other shires counties*

LONDON,

Printed by *R.O.* and *G.D.* for *Henry Overton,* 1642.

Title; Instructions for the Lieutenants

NEVV
ENGLANDS
FIRST FRUITS;

IN RESPECT,

First of the
{
Converſion of ſome,
Conviction of divers,
Preparation of ſundry
}
of the *Indians*.

2. Of the progreſſe of *Learning*, in the *Colledge* at CAMBRIDGE in *Maſſacuſets* Bay.

WITH
Divers other ſpeciall Matters concerning that *Countrey*.

Publiſhed by the inſtant requeſt of ſundry Friends, who deſire to be ſatisfied in theſe points by many *New-England* Men who are here preſent, and were eye or eare-witneſſes of the ſame.

Who hath deſpiſed the Day of ſmall things. Zach. 4. 10.

If thou wert pure and upright, ſurely now he will awake for thee : -- And though thy beginnings be ſmall, thy latter end ſhall greatly encreaſe. Iob. 8 6,7.

LONDON,
Printed by R. O and G. D. for *Henry Overton*, and are to be ſold at his Shop in *Popes-head-Alley.* 1 6 4 3.

Title; New Englands First Fruits

town deputy, prorogued the session. Through Bewitt the plaintiff promptly filed an angry protest, accusing Robert Williams of having summarily dissolved the court and protesting that since Williams was both Smith's bail and presiding officer of the court, he, Almy, was not likely to get a fair trial.

Smith, meanwhile, had become enraged at the action of Bewitt in having him, the president of the colony, arrested. He and his political ally, Samuell Gorton, general assistant from Warwick, filed an indictment charging Bewitt with high treason. Their action called for a General Assembly, to hear the case. It was held at Warwick, commencing 20 December 1652 and lasting six days, the longest session of the General Assembly up to that time and for many years thereafter.

The commissioners from Providence were Thomas Angell, Henry Brown, William Wickenden, James Ashton, Bewitt himself, and Gregory Dexter. In the first test of strength Dexter was elected moderator. Then Thomas Harris, a veteran politician, replaced James Ashton, who was absent, among the Providence commissioners. A letter was sent to Smith, requesting his presence so that he could explain "the weighty considerations invested in your warrant." Then, after the indictment had been read and Bewitt remanded into the custody of one Richard Townsend, the court adjourned to the next day.

Dexter was chosen moderator for each successive day of this tense assembly. How hotly the debates may have raged we have no way of knowing, for the records are mere skeletal reports of such orders as letting the prisoner go with his custodian to dinner at the ordinary, letting him be represented by counsel, sending men to take the testimony of a nearby housewife, calling again for the warrant, choosing a general sergeant *pro tem*, etc.

On the third day the trial paused long enough for the Assembly to pass a new law forbidding the arrest of a general officer of the colony in any case "betwixt party and party"; a summons was ordered to be sufficient. Passage of this act may have been a compromise measure, to prevent any recurrence of this trying situation.

However that may be, at the fourth day's session, on 23 December, Bewitt was acquitted, the Assembly stating that "Wee...cannot find the sayd Hugh Bewitt, prisoner, to have done, or attempted any grievous offence against the power and authoritie of that honourable State, the Commonwealth of England..." Bewitt was ordered restored to his place in the Assembly.[1]

For two days following Bewitt's acquittal the Assembly continued to sit, with Dexter still serving as moderator, and passed legislation of a varied sort.

No one not familiar with the difficulties of maintaining any semblance of order in the government of Providence

[1] The documents in the Bewitt case are to be found in *R. I. Col. Recs.*, I, 250-257 and scattered through Vol. XV of the *Prov. Recs.* They have been gathered in one place by Richard LeBaron Bowen in *The Providence Oath of Allegiance and Its Signers: 1651-2* (Providence, 1943).

Once cleared of the treason charge Bewitt pressed Almy's case against Smith with renewed vigor. The matter was heard at a town court of trials on 7 March 1652/3. Henry Reddock was added to the deputies in response to Almy's complaint against Robert Williams. Almy won a verdict, by default, Smith failing to appear either in person or by attorney. The jury awarded Almy £ 39/10/oo damages, plus costs of court, a total of £ 44/19/8. On 16 March, the sum not having been paid in to town clerk Dexter, an order was issued to Bewitt to seize £ 49/10/6 in lands or goods belonging to Smith, the additional sum being two shillings per pound to Bewitt for serving the execution.

It was at this Court of Trials on 7 March 1652/3 that an oath of allegiance to the Commonwealth of England, "as it is now established, without a king or House of Lords," was drawn up by Dexter and signed by him and eleven others. The signers may have been the jury in the Almy-Smith case, for, as such, they would have been required by an act of Parliament to take this oath.

William Dyer had returned from England in February 1652/3 and had written to Providence on the 18th of that month saying that he had "letters and orders concerning this colony." One of these probably contained the information which is to be found in a document on p. 7 of vol. I of the Rhode Island Historical Society Manuscripts. This document states that an oath of allegiance to the Commonwealth is required of all persons "that now doe, or shall any time hereafter act as members of any committee...under or by vertue of any Act or Ordinance of parliament...[etc.]"

The old style of dating has caused some confusion about the actual date of this oath, but this is dispelled by the fact that Thomas Wallin was sergeant, although absent, at this 7 March court, and he was not elected to that office until 7 June 1652, as is shown in *Prov. Recs.*, II, 63-64.

Plantations at this period can properly estimate the compliment paid to Dexter by his fellows when they chose him as moderator for these meetings. In either public regard or political power—the reader may choose his own interpretation—Dexter had neared his zenith among the inhabitants of the mainland towns. He actually reached that zenith the following May, when the commissioners from the mainland towns, sitting at Providence on the 16th and 17th, elected him president of the colony.

Dexter had also been chosen moderator of this meeting. It had important business to consider. Since the return of William Dyer from England in February with the news that Coddington's commission had been suspended, negotiations had been under way to re-establish the union of the four towns. A General Assembly had been held at Pawtuxet, half way between Providence and Warwick, on 25 February 1652/3, with Dexter as moderator. Its principal business was to draw up a reply to a proposal from Newport for a meeting of delegates from island and mainland to consider reunion. Four men were to go from the mainland, the two from Providence being Dexter and Bewitt.

Nothing was accomplished at this meeting, the mainland delegates reported on 9 March, after their return. They said they had not been allowed to see the instructions that Dyer brought, although many persons on the Island had seen them. There is no date known of this conference between island and main, but it probably took place on or before 1 March 1652/3, since the Island towns had met that day and reinstated those officials who were in office when Coddington's commission had arrived. Further there is the evidence that the mainland delegates picked up word of the need for an oath of allegiance to the Commonwealth at this meeting, for such an oath was taken at Providence on 7 March 1652/3 and in Warwick the following day.

At any rate, while the Island assembly set the first Tuesday after 15 May as the date for an election of new officers, the mainland faction offered to send commissioners on 10 days' notice. At the mainland court on 17 May they reported that there had been no response from the Island to this offer and the commissioners from Providence and Warwick decided to elect their own colony officers, as they had for the past two years, and Dexter was chosen president of the colony of Providence Plantations.

This same election kept Bewitt in his old office of general sergeant. The Dexter-Bewitt coalition was in full command, and John Smith and Samuell Gorton, who had sent a snappy letter to Providence, appealing from the decision made by the commissioners the previous December, when the Bewitt case was tried, were ordered to appear before a General Assembly in October at Warwick "to give answer for their sayd writinge and charge against the Court of Commissioners, and for their misdemeanours in their foresayd offices."[1] Bewitt, termed Solicitor General, an office he had held before the Coddington usurpation, was —with political, if not divine, irony—ordered to prepare "all the matter for tryall."

Apparently the case went no further, however, which was probably just as well for all concerned. Other matters of more importance claimed the attention of the mainland government; it still had reunion with the Island to consider and also preparations for defense against any attack by the Dutch.

At the Island election in May, William Dyer, Capt. John Underhill, and Edward Hull were given commissions to operate against the Dutch. This latter action alarmed the mainland and a General Assembly of Commissioners met at Providence 3 and 4 June 1653 to draw up a remonstrance against such a headstrong step, which they regarded as likely "to set all New England on fire" with a Dutch war. The Warwick and Providence commissioners explicitly recorded that this granting of commissions to Underhill, Hull, and Dyer in the name of Providence Plantations barred those responsible from taking part in the colony government "untill they give satisfaction to the respective Townes of Providence and Warwicke."

Further trouble for Dexter's administration arose at a court of commissioners in Warwick 13 August 1653. With

[1] *R. I. Col. Recs.*, I, 263. Mention of the Smith-Gorton letter is in *Prov. Recs.*, II, 68-69.

Dexter as moderator the meeting was called upon to consider a complaint from Stukeley Westcott, general assistant from Warwick, who asked that his town be ordered to go about choosing town officers. This was done, the court issuing the necessary order. This was the last of the attempts by the mainland government to operate separately from the Island. The sheer weight of the Island leaders was too much for them, and the court at Warwick adjourned at the call of either general assistant, never to be convoked again. The next meeting of commissioners was to be one attended by all four towns.

There are signs that some of the prominent mainland men were being won over to the Island's side. For instance, at a General Assembly held 16 May 1654 on the Island, Thomas Olney was elected general assistant for Providence, and he and "Mr. Williams" were named to a committee to prepare "a way of some course concerning our dissenting friends." Whether this was Roger or Robert Williams cannot be determined, but Roger was not yet back from England, as the records of this session show, although it is apparent that he was expected shortly.

Although the fact that Olney recognized the Island government may have shown which way the wind was blowing, the decisive factor in reuniting Island and mainland was the return of Roger Williams. With him he brought a letter from Sir Henry Vane, written at Williams' behest and chiding the colony severely for its divisions and quarrels. Williams supplemented it with one of his own, addressed to Gregory Dexter, who was still town clerk.[1] The letter, one of the finest Williams ever wrote, was obviously intended for all the townspeople, for in it he urged them to withdraw the remonstrance of June, 1653, and to obliterate the order denouncing the commissions issued to Dyer, Hull, and Underhill.

These two letters, coupled with the ardor with which Williams argued his case in private conversations, turned the tide in favor of reunion, and on 31 August 1654 commissioners from all four towns signed articles of agreement for the reuniting of the colony. Gregory Dexter was one of

[1] Staples, *Annals*, pp. 99.

the six who signed for Providence. The day the agreement was signed the commissioners started sessions at Warwick. At the session on 1 September Dexter was moderator; the court adjourned to 12 September after handling routine matters. On 10 September a town meeting was held in Providence and a slate nominated for general officers at the coming election. The choices were Roger Williams for president, Arthur Fenner and Thomas Harris for assistant, Dexter for recorder, Bewitt for sergeant, and John Sayles for general treasurer. Once more Gregory Dexter was a commissioner when the court met at Warwick on the 12th. Serving with him were Thomas Harris, "Mr. Henry" Reddock, William Wickenden, John Brown, and Henry Brown. In the voting Roger Williams was elected president and Thomas Harris was chosen assistant for Providence, but the other three Providence nominees, including Dexter, were defeated by a trio of Island men. Instead of becoming recorder Dexter was asked to serve with Roger Williams in drawing up and sending "letters of humble thanksgiving to the Lord Protector and Sir Henry Vane, Mr. [Cornelius] Holland, and to Mr. John Clarke, in ye name of ye Collonie."[1]

Seldom after this did Dexter serve the colony government. He was runner-up for the post of assistant from Providence in the election on 22 May 1655, but he was not a commissioner to that assembly. That same year he was one of 42 Providence inhabitants on the colony's first roll of freemen. When the charter granted by King Charles II finally arrived in 1663, Dexter was one of 26 colonists specifically mentioned by name, a distinction which marked him as one of Rhode Island's leading citizens. He was a deputy in the General Assembly which sat in October, 1664, and again in October, 1666. After that he appears

---

[1] *R. I. Col. Recs.*, I, 281-283. On 27 August 1654, the town of Providence had replied to Vane in a letter ostensibly written and signed by Dexter as town clerk, but the literary style is Roger Williams' and the historian Backus, who had apparently seen the original, said it was in Williams' hand. Williams did this same thing on other occasions, once when Thomas Olney, Jr., was town clerk. The letter to Vane is in *R. I. Col. Recs.*, I, 287. It should not be mistaken for Dexter's work.

in the colonial government only once and on that occasion as a sort of "elder statesman." That was when the General Assembly in April, 1676, faced with the crisis of King Philip's War, asked for the advice of Dexter and several others as "most juditious inhabitants."

How can we account for Dexter's disappearance from the colony government? He continued to serve the town, although not as prominently as during Roger Williams' absence, and, although seldom holding office, he was an active leader in the Williams-Fenner-Dexter faction which opposed the Harris-Olney-Whipple forces in the land disputes which I shall presently discuss.

Possibly he had fallen into disfavor during the time of the schism between the Island and the mainland. In a letter written more than ten years later Roger Williams hints that Dexter had voluntarily withdrawn from certain classes of office for reasons of conscience.

A more plausible reason, and one which possibly fits into Williams' picture of the man of conscience, would be Dexter's increasing activity as a Baptist minister. According to the historians of the Providence Baptist church, Dexter was ordained as minister of the First Baptist Church in 1655. Within a few years the Quakers had risen to power in the colonial government, and there was but little love between them and certain of the Providence Baptists. Such a situation might have resulted in Dexter's voluntary withdrawal, or, even more likely, it might have excluded him from major affairs.

XIV

THE CHASMORE EPISODE

GREGORY DEXTER and Roger Williams had a falling-out in 1656 and 1657, all due to an alleged affair between one Richard Chasmore of Pawtuxet and a heifer.

The case involved jurisdiction over Pawtuxet, where the Arnold faction's subjection to Massachusetts Bay was still technically in force. When word reached Williams, who was president of the colony, that two Indians had seen Chasmore practicing the *ars amatoria* on his heifer at Pawtuxet and that Chasmore's neighbors had concealed their knowledge of the crime, Williams promptly wrote to Massachusetts to ask what the authorities there intended to do about this and other charges of irregularities at Pawtuxet.

Some time earlier Williams had begun negotiations with the Bay for the return of Pawtuxet, and in these reports of varied immorality in the Massachusetts "suburb" he found further reasons for the course he advocated. Briefly, he argued that Massachusetts should either keep order at Pawtuxet or return the territory to Providence Plantations and let that colony end an intolerable situation. Williams' negotiations were progressing fairly well when Chasmore, after a brief flight to the Dutch, appeared at Williams' house in Providence late in September, 1656, and surrendered to the authorities. This made the position of Williams extremely difficult. He hesitated to proceed in the Rhode Island courts against Chasmore because the alleged offense had taken place in territory under the jurisdiction of Massachusetts. Eventually he discovered what appeared to be a way out; instead of holding Chasmore for trial he placed him under bonds to appear at Newport at a general court the following May, when the matter of jurisdiction could be decided by the colony officials. At the same time he turned down a request from Chasmore's friends for a trial at the March court of trials. He knew Chasmore had been advised to follow this course because of the difficulty of convicting on Indian testimony in the Rhode Island courts.

The legal picture became complicated indeed. The offense was allegedly committed under Massachusetts jurisdiction; Chasmore claimed he was not a Pawtuxet resident and was entitled to trial within the jurisdiction of Providence Plantations where "hath my reproaches beene raised"; and Williams maintained, as usual, an eye on the larger issue involved, which was to get Pawtuxet back into the fold and to avoid a clash with Massachusetts which might upset all the negotiations.

THE
Churches Refurrection,
OR THE
OPENING OF THE
Fift and sixt verfes of the 20th. CHAP.
OF THE
REVELATION.

By that Learned and Reverend,

IOHN COTTON
Teacher to the Church of BOSTON in
NEVV ENGLAND, and there corrected
by his own hand.

LONDON:
Printed by *R.O & G.D.* for HENRY OVERTON,
and are to be fold at his Shop in *Popes-head-Alley,*
1642.

Title; The Churches Resurrection

Church-Government

AND

Church-Covenant

DISCVSSED,

In an Anſwer of the Elders of the ſeverall Churches in
NEW-ENGLAND
To two and thirty Queſtions, ſent over
to them by divers Miniſters in *England*, to declare their judgments therein.

Together with an Apologie of the ſaid Elders in
New-England for Church-Covenant, ſent over
in Anſwer to Maſter *Bernard* in the
yeare 1639.

As alſo in an Anſwer to nine Poſitions about Church-
Government.

And now publiſhed for the ſatisfaction of all who deſire
reſolution in thoſe points.

LONDON,
Printed by *R.O.* and *G.D.* for *Benjamin Allen,*
Anno Dom. 1643.

Title; Church Government Discussed

Massachusetts, displaying its positive genius for stepping in at the wrong time, sent a couple of peace officers to Providence on 23 February 1656/7 to bring Chasmore back to the Bay. Providence's reaction was just as characteristic. The town rose as a man, precipitately called an illegal town meeting that same night, and, after treating the Massachusetts officers in somewhat cavalier fashion, took their prisoner away from them. And who should be on his feet at this meeting, clamoring the Providence side of the case, but Gregory Dexter. Richard Wait, the Bay's marshal, reported on the episode thus:

"...then rises vp one Dexter and said I desire to speake my consence and to stand for our liberty: Pawtucksitt is in our liberties and not in the bays....Dexter he stands vp againe and said Mr. President as he is our prisnor I stand for our libertye-deliuer him to the cunstabl: so herevppon Fenner he commanded the cunstabl to carry him away: Nay saith Dexter thet there be a mittimus maid and send him to Nue Port prison."

This action by the town was too much for Williams. A serious breach was opened between him and six men, including Dexter and his own son-in-law, John Sayles, against all of whom he presented charges, at the courts of trials in March and October, of being "ringleaders of factions, or new divisions," in violation of a colony law which had been enacted in 1655. But in characteristic fashion, when the time came for the trial, Williams was not in court—apparently on purpose—and the men were cleared for want of prosecution.[1]

Gregory Dexter had a few other contacts with the courts. On 26 June 1655 he served on both the grand inquest and the petit jury at a general court of trials in

[1] The documents in the Chasmore case are widely scattered. They are in *R. I. Col. Recs.*, I; *R. I. Court Recs.*, I; *Prov. Recs.*, II and XV; *Warwick Recs.; R. I. H. S. Publications*, VIII; *N. E. Hist. & Gen. Register*, VIII and XXXVI; Suffolk County (Mass.) Court files; John Carter Brown Library manuscripts; and R. I. Historical Society Manuscripts. They have been gathered in Bradford F. Swan, *The Case of Richard Chasmore alias Long Dick* (Providence, 1944). They should be read against the evidence of similar troubles in the Massachusetts jurisdiction, contained in the histories written by Governors John Winthrop and William Bradford.

Portsmouth, and in June, 1658, he was fined 10 shillings for failing to report for jury duty at a court in Newport.

During these years we find many minor references to him in the Providence town records. He and Thomas Harris were appointed by the town on 7 December 1652 to lay out a highway by Edward Inman's house. About 19 March 1654/5 he got an additional six acres of land.

By this time a bridge had been built across the Moshassuck to the west of his home-lot. It is frequently referred to in the records as Dexter's Bridge or "Mr. Dexter's" bridge, indicating that he owned it. This was the town's first bridge, it would seem, preceding the span across the Providence River at Market Square, and was used to get across to the meadow lands and common which lay between the Woonasquatucket and the Moshassuck. All the evidence indicates that it was a private bridge; there is no mention of its upkeep by the town nor of fixing tolls.

Some time before 20 April 1659 Dexter had helped Joseph Torrey, a refugee from Rehoboth, to fell timber for fencing and building on Torrey's lot in Providence, and at some indefinite date but probably early in his Providence career he and Thomas Angell were appointed fence-viewers. Gregory Dexter was carrying on the normal existence of a man in an average primitive settlement in New England.[1]

XV

DEXTER APPLIES A PLASTER

THE FRIENDSHIP between Gregory Dexter and Roger Williams was too strong to remain disrupted for long by the Chasmore case. Through the years Williams had depended on his old friend for many things, from printing to political support, and even for looking after Mrs. Williams and the children while he was away in England.

---

[1] The earliest mention of Dexter's Bridge that I have found is 27 January 1656/7, in *Prov. Recs.*, II, 99. All other references to Dexter's activity at this time can be found in *Prov. Recs.*, II and XV.

DEXTER APPLIES A PLASTER

On that occasion, in 1652, Williams concluded a letter to Dexter in truly touching words:

"Sr in this regard & when my publike Busines is ouer: I am resolved to begin my old Law Suite, so yt I haue no Thoughts of Returne vntill Spring Come twelue month. My Dutie & Affection hath Compelled me to acquaint my poore Companion with it: I Consider or many Children, ye danger of ye Seas & enemies & therefore I write not positiuely for her Only I acquaint her with or Affaires, I tell her how joyfull I should be of her being here with me vntill our Affaires were ended, & I freely leaue her to wait vpon ye Lord for Direction, & according as she finds her Spirit free & Chearfull So to Come or stay: Sr if it please ye Lord to giue her a free Spirit to cast her Selfe vpon the Lord I doubt not of yor Lo: & faythfull Care in any thing she hath occasion to vse yor helpe Concerning or Cheldren & Affaires during or Absence: but I Conclude, Whome I haue in Heaven, or Earth but Thee, & so humbly & thanckfully joy in ye Lords pleasure as only & infinitly best & sweetest."[1]

It was well that Williams had a man of Dexter's ability and integrity as a friend, for soon the great land dispute was to be joined, and with the wily William Harris as his principal adversary, Williams had need of all the help he could get. Somehow these two formed an alliance with Arthur Fenner, whose main interests in the past seem to have been military. Fenner was no idealist, in the sense that Williams and Dexter were, but he saw eye-to-eye with them in the land troubles, and this combination of Fenner, former lieutenant under Cromwell; Williams, college-trained minister, and Dexter, educated printer and experienced fighter of political battles, finally balked Harris in his scheme to set up a huge landed domain in the Rhode Island colony.

The land disputes had their beginning in the Pawtuxet Agreement to which I alluded in an earlier chapter. This agreement was the outgrowth of differences of opinion between Williams and the other original proprietors of Providence as to the handling of the land which had been granted to them by the Narragansett sachems. Williams wanted the land to be kept as a sort of trust, with the

---

[1] *Prov. Recs.*, XV, 62.

original proprietors sharing it with any persons whom they approved who sought refuge there. The proprietors, on the other hand, looked upon their settlement as their own proprietary right, a source of future wealth and income.

In an attempt at compromise Williams agreed to set aside part of the original Indian grant, that part known as Pawtuxet, to be the property of "the first monopolizing twelve," as he called them. Williams himself, one of the 13 original proprietors, accepted a 1/13th share in the Pawtuxet lands. This agreement had but little importance for many years after the colony was founded. During those years Pawtuxet included only a small area, and there was no idea that it might suddenly become larger.

It is true that the division was the basis of the first serious controversy in the community when an attempt was made to fix the exact boundaries of Pawtuxet. The Combination of 1640 took up the question of the north line of Pawtuxet in its first article and agreed that the dividing line ran indefinitely westward "betweene the two fresh Rivers [of] pautuxett: and wanasquatucket: of an even distance..." The vagueness of this description is readily apparent; trying to decide exactly what it meant resulted eventually in the bitterest schism in Providence's early history. This did not happen, however, until two things had made possible the westward expansion of Pawtuxet.

In May, 1658, Massachusetts finally relinquished its jurisdiction over Pawtuxet and the territory thereby became once more a part of Providence's jurisdiction, although naturally the title to the land itself remained in possession of the thirteen original owners, their heirs or assigns. Then, on 17 May 1659, the General Assembly gave Providence permission to clear out any Indians still living within its bounds and to purchase more land, up to three thousand acres, adjoining its borders.

For a couple of years the town itself did nothing to take advantage of this permission to purchase more land. But meanwhile William Harris, dwelling at Pawtuxet, had been more active. Within two weeks after the Assembly acted he began getting deeds from the sachems for a vast tract of land running inland twenty miles up the rivers.

These, instead of being straight deeds of sale, were confirmation deeds, giving to the men of Providence and to the men of Pawtuxet clear title to lands which, under the original grant, they had been allowed to use only in the sense that if their cattle strayed beyond the town's boundaries it would not be regarded as trespass. This right, contained in a memorandum added to the Town Evidence, as the first grant was called, stated that "up the Streame of pawtuckett and Pawtuxett without limmetts we might have for our use of Cattle." The phrase was commonly shortened to "upstream without limits" in the town debates.

Whatever the exact legal force of this clause might have been—and plenty of lawyers, from Harris down to the present century, have taken turns at interpreting it—the historian in drawing his conclusions must consider the intent behind it, and that intent is very clearly expressed by Roger Williams himself, who should have known the facts. Williams insisted that it meant that the town "being shortened in bounds by the sachem because of Indians about us, it might be no offense if our few cows fed up the rivers where nobody dwelt and home again at night."

Such was its meaning to an idealistic and honest man not looking for legal loopholes. But to the legalistic mind of William Harris a conveyance was a conveyance, whether the Indians knew what they were doing when they signed it or not. No scruples over *intent* ever restrained Harris; if the law said the land had been deeded to the white men, even if that law was completely beyond the comprehension of the Indians who made the grants, Harris could see no reason for not taking advantage of the situation.

There is no doubt about his taking that advantage. His three confirmation deeds added not three thousand acres to the town but three hundred thousand acres! Furthermore, these deeds were slyly worded. The first one not only confirmed to the English the land for twenty miles upstream "for their use of cattle" but also "for Sumer and Winter feeding of their Cattle; and plowing and all other Nessesarey Jmprovements, as for farmes, and all Manner of plantation whatso Ever"; the other two deeds were much the same.

85

When the town, at a "packed" meeting on 26 March 1660, ordered its western bounds set at twenty miles west from Foxes Hill in the heart of the village, trouble began to occur. The strife became increasingly bitter when Harris, in behalf of the Pawtuxet proprietors, sought to have the dividing line between their special preserve and the town's common lands, first fixed in the Combination of 1640, run from its somewhat indefinite end westward to the twenty-mile limit. The course this line was to take was of the greatest importance. If it continued in a generally westward direction at an equal distance between the Pawtuxet and Woonasquatucket rivers, as originally agreed, the Pawtuxet lands would become a vast domain, for the line, in remaining equidistant between the two streams, would curve northward, making Pawtuxet bigger the farther inland it went.

To at least three men of Providence the enormity of Harris' land-grabbing scheme was readily apparent. Roger Williams, who all his life stood for honest dealings with the Indians, could not allow it to go through unopposed; to him it was the perpetration of a gigantic fraud on the Indians, a betrayal which would irreparably lower the standing of the white man and his God in Indian eyes.

Gregory Dexter's opposition is not so easy to explain. Supporters of Harris have laid it to his cantankerous disposition and love of argument. I feel, lacking any evidence to the contrary, that, like Williams, he opposed the scheme on moral grounds. Certainly we must remember that he was a Baptist minister at this time, and, if Williams is to be believed, his famous tender conscience was then functioning full blast.

Whatever arrayed Arthur Fenner beside these two men is even less explicable. Perhaps it was what we would call today the "party line," and Fenner, as a leader of the Williams-Dexter faction in other matters, joined with them in this cause, too. Such reasoning, however, would hardly explain the ardor with which Fenner fought for the cause, nor would it account for the abuse, in and out of court, to which he submitted without the slightest sign of reluctance.

To the
READER.

I T is not hard to believe that such discourses as this wil meet with divers censures, the prophane and ignorant loathing Christ, and any thing concerning him; the Formalist accounting such truths troublesom that may ingage him in the change of his opinions and practises, and some of the wisest will be apt to question the tyming such light as this : yea doubtles this pamphlet-glutted age will so looke upon it, and lay it by.

But because I doe conceive that this sword will not be sheath'd which is now drawn, till Church-work be better known, and more countenanced, and since safety is laid up in the Temple, Psa. 27. 3,4,5. I could not but help on this, which attended and practised may prove our security next to Christ. These were either sudden answers to our doubting and inquiring Brethren, or some satisfaction rendred about our so much slighted Church-Covenant, which wee could not but thinke might come to view, for the present stay to some faithfull soules, that call for light, and intend to use it well : for others, of what kind soever, we must beare their hard or thoughts, among those usuall loads of scandals, that men of our judgement must carry, especially if zeale for the Truth draw them forth to publike observation; nor doe we purpose (God helping us) to succumbe under calumny, being the livery of quieter times then these, let us bee viler still, so God and his Arke may be more glorious. Yet this I doe professe for my selfe and Brethren that as we have not bin dealt with, nor convinc'd of any offence; so we shall ever be ready to give an account of that hope which is in us, being call'd thereunto; in the meane time we over looke these barkings of black mouthes, and wish a good Comment be made upon the text of our plaine meaning.

The onely way I know to reach Gods mind in Worship will bee to love the truth for it's owne sake : yea to love it when it shall condemne our practises and persons also : Who hath not observed that the first step to error is the declining the truth in love to it ?

Hence

Text; Church Government Discussed

A KEY into the

LANGUAGE

OF

AMERICA:

O R,

An help to the *Languige* of the *Natives*
in that part of A M E R I C A, called
NEW-ENGLAND.

Together, with briefe *Obfervations* of the Cu-
ftomes Manners and Worfhips, &c. of the
aforefaid *Natives*, in Peace and Warre,
in Life and Death.

On all which are added Spirituall *Obfervations*,
Generall and Particular by the *Authour*, of
chiefe and fpeciall ufe (upon all occafions.)to
all the *Englifh* Inhabiting thofe parts ;
yet pleafant and profitable to
the view of all men :

BY ROGER WILLIAMS
of *Providence* in *New-England*.

LONDON,
Printed by *Gregory Dexter*, 1643.

Title; *A Key into the Language of America*

Williams, in a letter to John Whipple, Jr., on 24 August 1669, points out that originally Fenner had been on Harris' side, along with William Wickenden, but that "God hath bene pleased to Pluck out these 2 & many others out of yt horrible Pit....As to Cap. Fenner, whether jt were ye Busines of a few Rajlers yt occasioned his breach with W. Har. (as some say)...or whether jt was W. Har: his base & reproachfull vsage of him when refusing to attest to some bounds (wch Arth: Fenner could not in Conscience yeald to,) he cald Arthur Fenner False fellow, Rouge & Rascall &c. (after all ye Service & Drudgerie Performed for him) or what euer else were ye occasion wch God was Pleased to awaken Cap: Fenner with...surely he came to be fully satisfied in his Soule & Conscience yt jt was not Publke Commonweale worck yt he had bene engaged in, but for W. Har: Private Ends, designs & Plots:"

At any rate and whatever their reasons the three men formed a solid front against Harris and for years fought a cause to which each, in his own way, was to make important contributions. The first strategy resorted to by the Williams faction was to ignore the whole idea of a twenty-mile westward expansion of Providence, despite the town's vote in favor of this plan and a subsequent vote, on 14 May 1660, to run the western boundary north and south from the Pawtucket (now Blackstone) River to the Pawtuxet River through a point seven miles due west of Foxes Hill. Several requests by Harris for the town to run the dividing line between Providence and Pawtuxet farther westward were quietly ignored or met with delaying tactics, and Harris was too busy with other suits against Warwick men and others of his neighbors, whom he regarded as trespassing upon his private domain, to press the matter in Providence town meeting.

It was not until 31 March 1665 that the town finally agreed to run the dividing line as far west as Hipses Rock. This landmark was one of the original bounds of the first grant from the sachems, and hence the step represented no real concession to Harris' demands. Furthermore, although there seems to have been an idea of carrying the line even farther west, it was agreed that if any difference of opinion developed as to where the line should run beyond the rock that question should be settled by arbitrators. The whole business was thus left in abeyance. Harris, whirling about from law-suit to law-suit, was winning verdicts but could not get executions.

A crisis arose, however, in the Providence town elections on 3 June 1667. Two town meetings were held that day, one called by Harris and his Pawtuxet partner, William Carpenter, and the other called by Fenner. Fenner called his meeting after the meeting sponsored by Harris had refused certain townsmen the right to vote, on the ground that they had not taken the oath of allegiance to the King, required of all voters, because they had taken it before Fenner who, they claimed, was not qualified to administer it. At both meetings town officers were elected and, at later meetings, two sets of deputies to the General Assembly. At the General Assembly in July at Newport the deputies elected by the Fenner meeting were seated and those chosen at the Harris meeting were rejected. Then Fenner was acquitted of Harris' charge of fomenting a rout. The Fenner faction took over management of the town's affairs, retaining that control for three years.

It was at the Fenner-controlled meeting on 3 June that Gregory Dexter's part in the conflict with Harris first became apparent. A paper written by Dexter was presented to the meeting by his nephew, Thomas Clemence, and was ordered placed on the records. This paper, which enunciated an official position for the town to take on the land questions, has been popularly known ever since as the Sovereign Plaster or as Dexter's Plaster. Its full title is:

Salus Poppuli [Suprema Lex, or] The Health of the people the [Supreme] Law. An Jnstrument, or soueraign Plaister, to heale the many fold prsant soares in this Towne or plantation of prouidence, wch doe arise about lands: and to pruent the furder spreading of them boath amongst orselues, & ye whole Colony: Necesserey forthwith to be jmproued and applyed, least this Towne should fall into Griuouss sores or Gangrenes to the hurt of the whole Colony: & therby this Towne which was ye first in this Bay, become the worst and that (only) about lands in the wildernes

pr   Gregory Dexter

DEXTER APPLIES A PLASTER

For fifty years a gross slander against Dexter has been current in Rhode Island history. Henry C. Dorr, when he wrote *The Proprietors of Providence, and Their Controversies with the Freeholders* (*R. I. H. S. Collections*, vol. IX) (Providence, 1897), charged that Dexter had secretly entered this paper in the records fourteen years before the date on which it was presented to the town meeting. Dorr contended this secret and illegal entry took place in 1653, when Dexter was town clerk.

It is about time that this wrong against Dexter was righted. There is not a shred of evidence to support Dorr's allegation, except the chronological position of the document among the records as they now are. The book in which it was written had fallen apart before 1800 and the pages were badly jumbled in rebinding.[1] Furthermore, the book originally contained such foundation documents as the Combination of 1640, now missing, and the Twenty-Five Acre Men's Agreement, and thus would have been the natural place to record such a statement of policy. But, worst of all, Dorr failed to examine the original, or, if he did so, failed to notice what is perfectly obvious: that the Plaster is not in Gregory Dexter's handwriting. The writing is that of Shadrach Manton, and Shadrach was elected town clerk at this 3 June meeting. It would be stretching credulity beyond the breaking point to contend that Dexter, with the town books in his possession in 1653, had taken the trouble to have Shadrach Manton write the document into them as a means of deception.

Apparently the veil of Dorr's hatred for Dexter was lifted long enough for him to be puzzled by the internal evidence of the document, for it mentions events which had not occurred and situations which had not come up until several years after 1653. But Dorr brushed aside any doubts he may have entertained concerning the Plaster's date and declared that it must have been revised to make it conform with conditions in 1667!

This is a remarkable example of the extremes to which an historian will sometimes go to support an assumed posi-

[1] The wide outer margins were sewn together to form the inner hinges of the rebound book, which consequently has to be read backwards most of the time.

tion. Dorr, for some reason, made Dexter the villain of his entire piece, even going so far as to declare that the Plaster was written in language of "so harsh a character" that Williams was careful, in discussing it, "to restrain his approval to the 'proposals' of Dexter, saying nothing about their language." Considering that Williams, in a letter written for the town on 31 August 1668, accused Harris of having "lickt vp his vomit," among other things, and is famous for the heat he could generate in the prose of a philippic, Dorr's observation is nothing short of ludicrous.[1]

As a matter of fact, Dexter's Plaster, far from being a diatribe, was rather calm in its language, although its proposals must have been anathema to Harris and his party. Its sub-title may have been colorful, but it was hardly extraordinary by the standards of the London revolutionary pamphlets in the printing of which Dexter had had so much experience.

The Plaster's four proposals were a simple explanation of the Williams-Dexter-Fenner party's platform on the land question. The first proposal declared against any plan "to divide to the men of Pawtuxet 20 miles" as "unjust and unreasonable." The second proposal argued for strict adherence to the town bounds as expressed in the Town Evidence and stated more particularly "about twenty years since." It also elucidated the phrase "upstream without limits," taking its meaning to be that which Williams had always contended: a simple means of avoiding arguments over chance trespass by wandering cattle. The third section called for an equitable division of some lands to the westward, purchased in 1662 by Williams, Olney, and others. In these lands 25-Acre Men and Proprietors were to share equally if they had paid equal sums toward the cost of the purchase. The final proposal was a concession to the Proprietors, requiring the presence of at least twenty-one of them at any meeting at which lands within the *old* bounds were disposed of, exchanged, or recorded.

[1] Those desiring to examine Dorr's reasoning on the Sovereign Plaster are referred to *R. I. H. S. Collections*, IX, 66-72. The Plaster itself is in *Prov. Recs.*, II, 72-75.

AN
Helpe to the native Language
of that part of *America* called
N E W - E N G L A N D.

CHAP. I.
Of *Salutation*.

Observation.

HE Natives are of two forts, (as the
English are.) Some more Rude and
Clownifh, who are not fo apt to
Salute, but upon *Salutation* refalute
lovingly. Others, and the generall, are *fober*
and *grave*, and yet chearfull in a meane, and as
ready to begin a Salutation as to Refalute,
which yet the Englifh generally begin, out of
defire to Civilize them.

B   *What*

Text; A Key into the Language of America

Mr Cottons
LETTER
Lately Printed,
EXAMINED
AND
ANSVVERED:

By *Roger Williams* of *Providence*
In
NEW·ENGLAND.

LONDON,
Imprinted in the yeere 1644.

Title; Mr. Cottons Letter . . . Examined

These principles had the support of Roger Williams, for on 24 August 1669 he wrote to John Whipple, Jr.:

"What matter of force was there in Mr. Dexters 3 proposalls[1] for peace & Accomodatjon? Were they not honest, equall & peaceable to any yt minded not thejr owne Cabins more Then the Common Good of our poore tossed Barke & Vessell?"

William Harris, however, took a different view of Dexter's action. He saw Dexter and Fenner responsible, as leaders of their faction in town, for keeping him out of his lands, and from that day onwards he sought to hale them into court and force them to grant his demands. Harris was entirely justified in believing that Dexter was determined to prevent him and his Pawtuxet partners from acquiring the huge tract of land they wanted. Dexter's next move shows that.

At a meeting in William Wickenden's house on 21 January 1667/8, according to the testimony of two witnesses, Dexter proposed a declaration which he called "Equal Conclusions." The gist of this proposal was that "all those who would not subscribe to their agreements (the policies contained in the Sovereign Plaster?) but oppose" would have their lands outside the town bounds, as expressed in the Sovereign Plaster, liable to the disposal of a major part of the purchasers, who could easily outvote the 13 Proprietors and their followers. There was an exception, however, in that those who did not subscribe but nevertheless did not actively oppose the agreements would retain their lands. Whether these Equal Conclusions were the presentation from Dexter which the town on 26 February 1668/9 ordered kept among the records, or whether he offered another proposal on that date, we do not know, for nothing in the way of such a paper has survived.

When Harris contested the validity of the elections at the Fenner-controlled town meeting of 3 June 1667, and was turned down by the General Assembly, his whole scheme boomeranged. The Assembly held that he had not only put it to the trouble and cost of a special meeting but

[1] This may have been a slip on Williams' part, or it may refer to the Plaster and some other proposals.

then had also objected to the Assembly's decision. Therefore it fined him £50 and discharged him from his office of assistant. This had temporarily eclipsed the power of the Harris party in Providence, and the Fenner group ruled in town meetings until late in 1669.

In May, 1668, however, Harris was once more an assistant, by election of the General Assembly. In October of the same year his fine was remitted. It was easy to see that he was regaining favor with the colony authorities. A committee of Providence and Pawtuxet men ran the dividing line as far west as the Pocasset River, a short distance beyond Hipses Rock, in January, 1669, but that was the only concession made in the face of Harris' increasing strength.

Just what happened to overthrow the Fenner party at Providence in 1669 is not to be discovered in the existing records. On 5 April Fenner adjourned a town meeting to 27 April, but on 19 April a meeting was held with Thomas Olney as moderator and deputies were chosen for the coming General Assembly. Another meeting was held on 27 April, as scheduled, with Fenner as moderator, but the records make no mention of any deputies being chosen. From then on the town meetings, with Thomas Olney, Jr., as moderator, were under the sway of the Harris party. Harris promptly drew up an answer to the Sovereign Plaster and presented it to the town on 15 December 1669. Harris contended that the Plaster had been "unlawfully forced into ye Towne book," that its contents were illegal, and that it was "an evell instrument & poysonous plaster tending not to ye weal but wo of ye Towne...." The town agreed that the Plaster was "vtterly vnwholesome and jlleagall" and declared it wholly null and void.

But, on the other hand, Harris made no progress in the matter of the dividing line. Quite desperate over this continued thwarting of his scheme he began to look to Connecticut for possible help in getting the land he wanted. In 1672 he wrote a paper in which he attacked the Rhode Island Charter, saying that the Connecticut Charter gave that colony prior right to lands on the west shore of Narragansett Bay—including the lands which Harris desired to possess at all costs.

Roger Williams sprang into action and testified against Harris before the General Assembly, which forthwith ordered Harris arrested and jailed to await trial. In May, however, there was a complete change in the government, effected by a coalition between the Quakers and the pro-Connecticut element from the Narragansett country. Harris was released in time to attend the great debates between Williams and the Quakers at Newport in August, and later at Providence, and lost no time, according to Williams, in currying favor among the Quakers at both places.

All this time Harris had been conducting suits against his various opponents. But, failing to move the stubborn townsmen of Providence or to make any progress in those suits in which he had won judgments, Harris resorted to an appeal to the King in Council. He was in England for that purpose in the Spring of 1675, but although the King granted his petition and ordered the governors of the four New England colonies to hear the case before a jury drawn from the four colonies, King Philip's War prevented any immediate action. It was not until 17 November 1677 that this special court finally started actual hearings at Providence.

The Providence townsmen had met on 27 July 1677 and chosen Roger Williams, Gregory Dexter, and Captain Arthur Fenner "to draw up an Answer" to Harris' bill of complaints. On 25 August the three men presented this answer to the town and it was approved. The answer pointed out that since the recent "Great Judgements" of the Lord had not deterred Harris from "striving so vehemently about Lands, Lands," and since he claimed the King had "appointed a way (as you say) to end the said differences," the town stood ready "to give answer...according to the occasion."

On 13 and 15 October Harris and his partner, Thomas Field, filed with the court declarations against Mr. Gregory Dexter, Captain Arthur Fenner, and the town of Providence. The first declaration charged a trespass, in that Dexter and Fenner, through their party, had held up the running of the dividing line for "five or six years paste," and went on

93

to charge them with being "tenants by force." It asked £10 damages and the land claimed by the Harris partners.

The second declaration expatiated on the "methods" used by Dexter and Fenner; it charged them with being "active leading Instruments in carrying on a defference with divers persons after comers of ye sd town" by having had the sergeant summon the plaintiffs to town meetings "and there bid us for peace sake [to] relinquish our Claymes to a great parte of our land of patuxet as if they should suggest we wear like to have no peace, but by soe doeing..." Dexter and Fenner were also charged with having stirred up Warwick, and Dexter alone with having conspired to overthrow the Harris title so that he could force his way, along with his Providence party and a party from Rhode Island, into a 13-mile tract which would perforce encroach upon Pawtuxet.[1] Finally, the declaration asked once more that the dividing line be run as far inland as Ponagansett Pond, which Harris said was about 12 miles from the eastern bounds of Providence.

When the hearing opened on 17 November Harris presented a document which has since become known as the Plea of the Pawtuxet Purchasers. It was an all-inclusive charge, naming Dexter among several others and stating the case for Harris and his partners. Incidentally it announced that a copy of the Sovereign Plaster would be presented for examination.

On 27 October 1677 the town of Providence had chosen three men to answer Harris and, although no names are given in the record, Williams, Dexter, and Fenner filed the reply in behalf of the town. Evidently taking a cue from Harris, whose legal quibbling had won so many verdicts, the three men first filed a sort of demurrer, pointing out that although Harris had set forth in his petition to the Crown that he and twelve partners had bought Pawtuxet from the Indians he now said in his declaration that he

---

[1] Harris' phraseology here is so vague that I cannot state definitely what he is driving at. Anyone desiring to have a try at untangling the mystery is referred to *R. I. H. S. Collections*, X, 200 or 217. Perhaps some key document has been lost to us; or Harris may be talking about some rumored conspiracy.

QVERIES

OF HIGHEST

CONSIDERATION,

Propoſed to

Mr. *Tho. Goodwin* Mr. *Jer. Burroughs*
Mr. *Phillip Nye* Mr. *Sidr. Simpſon.*
Mr. *Wil. Bridges*

AND

To the Commiſſioners from the Generall
Aſſembly (ſo called) of the Church

OF

SCOTLAND;

Vpon occaſion of their late Printed Apologies for
themſelves and their *Churches.*

In all Humble Reverence preſented to the view
of the Right Honourable the Houſes of the
High Court of Parlament.

LONDON,
Imprinted in the yeare **MDCXLIV.**

Title; Queries of Highest Consideration

QUERIES
PROPOUNDED
To the five *Holland* Miniſters, and the *Scotch Commiſsioners*.

WORTHY SIRS,

N ſerious Examination of your late *Apologies*, we ſhall in all due reſpect and tenderneſſe humbly Querie :

First, What Precept or Pattern hath the Lord Jeſus left you in his laſt Will and Teſtament for your *Synod*, or Aſſembly of *Divines*, by vertue of which you may expect his *preſence* and *aſſiſtance*?

Querie I.
What warrant from the Lord Ieſus for the Aſſembly of Divines?

If you ſay (as all Popiſh *Synods* and Councels doe) the Pattern is plain, *Acts* 15. We aske if two or three Brethren of one particular Congregation at *Antioch*, ſent to that firſt Mother Church at *Jeruſalem*, where the Apoſtles were, who being (immediatly) inſpir'd from God, could ſay, *It ſeemeth good to the holy Spirit and Vs, to lay upon you no greater burthen*, &c. as alſo who had power to make Decrees for all the Churches, *Acts* 16. We aske whether this be a Pattern, for a Nation or Kingdome (and ſo conſequently for more Nations, and all the World. if under one Government, as in *Auguſtus Ceſars* tax) to ſend their ſeverall Prieſts and Deacons (for other ſpirituall Officers then Biſhops, Prieſts and Deacons you know we have not) to reforme or forme a Religion, *&c* ?

Acts 15. examined.

A Nationall Aſſembly neceſſarily inforceth an Aſſembly of the whole world.

We pray you to conſider, if the golden Image be not a type and figure of the ſeverall Nationall and State Religions, which all Nations ſet up, and Ours hath done, for which the wrath of God is now upon Us ?

Dan. 3.
Daniels Image, a type of State Religions.

We

Text; Queries of Highest Consideration

had bought Pawtuxet from Williams, "who is no Indian."
It also pointed out that Harris said in one place that Pawtuxet was bought from Williams for £20 and in another
that "it was not bought but given."

Dexter and Fenner also filed a lengthy answer to Harris'
declaration, and Williams subscribed his agreement "so
far as concerns the town for whom I was chosen one to
Answer." Dexter and Fenner answered Harris' charge of
illegal meetings by pointing out that the Assembly had
"justifyed them & owned their choice of deputies." As to
the conspiracy charge against Dexter, their answer was
that "If this were true, then Gregory Dexter would appeare
to all men that heares hereof [to] be a covetous man after
Land and vile: But this is not true, for it is a notorious
Slander, & he or they that uttereth slanders, is a————
what he is I leave to the Court to Judge, for I have neither
directly, nor indirectly any part in that 13 miles of land,
and now where are the Company of trespassers whereof
these men speak, by force to inforce their way, but as a
man is, so is his strength."

Dexter, obviously the author of this reply, goes on to
say that he could not claim his land "because I fear least
that saying come on me which is written, as a partridge
that setteth on her eggs & hatcheth them not, so he that
getteth goods (or land) and not by right, shall leave them
in the midst of his days & dye a fool."[1]

"Furthermore they say their title standeth upon Great
Rocks, and Argues largly," the answer continues. "We
answer your building is so high of 12 miles as you say, &
others say tis 20 that we dare not climb up with you, least
we fal, and split upon that rock of Eliz: 5 chapter against
fraudulent procurers of deeds & their accessories, see the
Law." The answer then states what is nowhere else mentioned: that Gregory Dexter was indicted by William
Harris, on the same charges of rioting which Harris brought
against Fenner, but in Governor Benedict Arnold's time,
and that the indictment was quashed.

As for that Pawtuxet which Harris was trying to claim,
the answer protested ignorance, but "as for that Pawtuxet

[1] The quotation is modified from Jeremiah, XVII, 11.

wch was given to or loving neighbor Williams, we know, we nor the Town hath not withheld from you, but have run a line or partion according to the arbitration or Combination, &c. Therefore to pray a remedy for this, you needed not, & so you have no cause to call up for damage at or or the Towns dore."

The final argument in the answer is remarkably sound, and the wonder is that it did not make a favorable impression on the men from the other colonies. It contended that if the twenty miles upstream were to apply to the westward then it would have to be applied all around, on the Pawtucket as well as on the Pawtuxet. And this meant that Warwick would have to give up land, so would two of Harris' partners and the men from Meshantatuck, all on the south part of the tract, while on the north Massachusetts would have to be persuaded to give up about eight miles "into their Patent" and some of Mendon's land on the west side of the Blackstone River, while Billings and Inman would have to "lay down" their purchases in northern Rhode Island.[1] "Not till then," the answer states, "will it be fair to talk of such a prtition to the men of Pawtuxet, wch when that is, we do not think to live to see." The town's spokesmen conclude by expressing willingness to refer to the jury the question whether the land either twelve or twenty miles inland was really the Pawtuxet which Harris had declared to the King in Council that he and his partners had bought from the Indians forty years before.

This answer was able in one sense: it took into account the weakness of the confirmation deeds and went behind them to the historical background of the situation. It was also firmly grounded in common sense. But it was weak in the sort of legal hair-splitting and trickery which then intrigued and titillated the judicial mind. In twenty years the issue of whether the confirmation deeds defrauded

---

[1] Apparently Harris had envisioned some such objection, which would account for his reducing his claims to twelve miles inland. For his contorted reasoning in arriving at a figure of twelve miles inland, the reader is invited to study the Plea of the Pawtuxet Purchasers, *R. I. H. S. Publications*, I, 185-213.

their grantors—by having them confirm a grant never actually made—had become lost in a wilderness of bickering. So early as 1677 there was a widespread willingness to leave to historians, as just an academic question, the problem of discovering what the sachems actually intended to convey to Roger Williams in the Town Evidence.

The Court took the practical view: Harris had the deeds; the deeds gave him the land he claimed. Therefore, had he been damaged by not being able to take possession? The jury's verdict said he had...£2 worth. Dexter, Fenner, and the town were to be assessed that amount in behalf of Harris and Field, plus costs of court. In addition the jury called for an order from the court to run the dividing line westward at an equal distance between the Pawtuxet and the Woonasquatucket until it met "with a thwart line from the head of Wenasquetucket River directly Runing to Pawtuxet River."

Dexter and Fenner appealed to the court on 22 November to set aside the verdict. They contended the town had not been sued by a "writ of partition" but for £10 damages, and that Harris had confessed he had never seen the rivers, "therefore why we should be damnified by walking ye wildernesse with him, judge ye."

Unmoved by this plea, the Court issued a warrant to George Way, town sergeant of Providence, to see that the verdict was carried out. But again Harris was balked, for Way returned the warrant the following June, saying that he had not executed it "because they had not agreed to prfect ye running of the foresaid lines."

Here Fenner's hand can be seen at work. Appointed on 24 December 1677 by the town to determine the head of the Woonasquatucket, he had found a way to defeat Harris through the vague wording of the verdict. In the first place there was the question of exactly what was meant by a direct line. And where was the head of the river? And did the verdict mean direct to the Pawtuxet or direct to its largest tributary, the Pocasset? Even Harris hesitated to answer some of these questions; he proposed arbitration. But his offer was ignored and on 19 June 1678 the jurors were ordered to be in Providence on 1 October to explain their verdict.

Meanwhile the town had accepted a report from Fenner's committee as to the location of the head of the river, and Fenner was empowered to engage John Smith, a surveyor, to run the thwart line. Fenner evidently coached Smith well for the first line the surveyor laid down not only gave Pawtuxet no increased area but actually cut off some territory which both sides had conceded for years to be part of the Pawtuxet tract. A second line was then run and it proved to be almost as bad. It ran from the Fenner-designated head of the Woonasquatucket—which was placed at the confluence of several small streams rather than at the actual source some distance farther inland—to the junction of the Pocasset and the Pawtuxet, and it added very little to the Pawtuxet territory.

Harris complained bitterly at these tactics. He had not forgotten the principles expressed in Dexter's Sovereign Plaster and when, on 23 May 1678, he wrote a protest against these two thwart lines he accused his Providence foes of still adhering to them. Despite this protest Harris was doomed to further disappointment. The Rhode Island members of the special court called for 1 October refused to take part in the proceedings on the ground that a Connecticut member had failed to appear; they raised the question whether the court were not dissolved on this account. Furthermore, the Rhode Island members of the jury, although they appeared, refused to do anything about explaining their verdict, contending that they had given the verdict, it had been accepted by the Court, and they had been dismissed. Thereupon the court's remaining members referred the whole matter to the King, thus delaying execution of the verdict for Harris. Once more the indefatigable litigant from Pawtuxet set sail for England to press his case before the King.

Gregory Dexter figures in the case only once more. Following Harris' successful appeal to the King, the Rhode Island governor and his council in 1679 ordered execution against Fenner, Dexter, and the town of Providence for £2 damages and £19/ 09/ 10 for costs of court. Harris, still hating Dexter, singled him out in his instructions to his attorneys for collecting this sum.

THE
BLOUDY
TENET,
OF PERSECVTION,
for cauſe of *CONCIENCE*,
diſcuſſed, in

A Conference *betweene*

TRVTH and PEACE,

WHO,
In all tender affection, preſent to the
High Court of PARLIAMENT, (as the
Reſult of their *Diſcourſe*) theſe, (amongſt
other *Paſſages*) of *higheſt conſideration*.

Printed in the Yeere 1644.

Title; The Bloudy Tenet, 1644

THE

BLOVDY TENENT,

of PERSECUTION, for caufe of
CONSCIENCE, difcuffed, in

A Conference *betweene*

TRVTH and PEACE.

VVHO,

In all tender Affection, prefent to the High
Court of *Parliament*, (as the *Refult* of
their *Difcourfe*) thefe, (amongft other
Paffages) of *higheft confideration.*

Printed in the Year 1644.

Title; *The Bloudy Tenent, second edition*

"And as to executution on theyr Cattell or Chattells for our Costs & damages," Harris wrote, "take not execution of any yt did not deny us our sd right line whose names are knowne but take execution only on Gregory Dexter & his party, & refuse ye Cattell of others If they be offered to you."

But Harris, though he won all the verdicts, still could not get a satisfactory execution in the matter of the dividing line. With astonishing persistence and undaunted in his efforts to get the vast tract of land he had dreamed of, in 1679 he set sail for England a third time. The ship was captured by Barbary pirates and Harris was taken as a slave to Algiers and there held for ransom. When this was paid two years later he finally made his way to London, but there he died at the home of a friend only three days after his arrival.

A last ironic twist is given to this tale by Arthur Fenner. On 16 December 1684, when he was a man in his sixties, he married Howlong Harris, daughter of his ancient enemy and by all accounts as headstrong as her father before her.[1]

For many years after Harris' death the struggle for the Pawtuxet lands raged on, but always with increasingly diminished bitterness. And in the end it was Dexter who won the posthumous victory.

[1] *Prov. Recs.*, XV, 233 and 231-233 give us an interesting little story about the romantic Howlong. On 29 June 1681 Mrs. Susan Harris wrote to Capt. Fenner and the other two assistants serving formal notice that she forbade any of them to "Joyne John pocoke and my Daughter Howlong Harris to geather in marrage: till I here from my Husband of his Consent to it and leagall publication: as law requireth: nor suffer them to take Each other before any of you: and doe Jmpower my frind and yours John Whipple junr to speake for me and my Husband in ye Case. . . . ."

Whether Whipple spoke up at this time we do not know but some time after 20 August 1681 he made a lengthy deposition in regard to Howlong's behavior. On that day, Whipple said, Howlong came to his house about noon and asked him to ride home with her. Whipple said he told her he would if he could get a horse. When he was unable to do so he invited her to spend the night, saying that he had a spare bed. Howlong allowed as how she didn't mind if she did stay all night, "for I have a Letter to write."

Whipple then offered her a bed in the chamber with his children and daughters but Howlong declined it and it was given, Whipple says, to "other persons." Howlong elected to sit up and write, and Whipple fetched her some candles and went to bed. Before daylight he was called to fetch some wine for a guest and then sat smoking his pipe until the sun rose. Howlong told him to go to bed so that she might finish her letter, and Whipple complied.

When he awakened after a nap he saw the chamber doors open, he said, and could hear conversation in the chamber where Howlong had gone, according to one of his daughters. It seems that one Tom Drew had joined her there. Whipple's deposition continues:

"Then I said where is Onseforus, ye garll sayd he is gon to my Grandfather Whipples; then this Deponant sayd where is Thomas: ye garll Answered I doe not know I did not see him: since he came out of ye new house Chamber . . . and then ye sayd Onesieforus: came in at ye other dore next to my fathers: and pased as I thought through ye roome at ye other Dore: and presently upon it I heard one say you shant, and another say I will, then I heard ye same words againe. . . .Then I called sayeing, Oneseforus come heith; soe he came to me to ye bedd side: then I sayd to him, that same fellow dissturbs Howlong: nameing ye words to him yt I heard, sayeing goe put him by; soe then he went up in to ye Chamber where they were and presently came downe againe and my little Boye with him, the which I knew not to be theire till he came downe with him ye said Onesefor: then ye sayd Oneseforuss asked me for a gill of rum I sayd I would fill it when I gott up, soe turning my back towards him: to taulke to my wife: he filled one for him selfe: (as often times he had done before) and went up into ye Chamber againe: and then ye sayd Oneseforus came downe againe, (with ye gill of Drink, or most of it in his hand) and Howlong, and ye sayd Thomas, ye sayd: Howlong passing out of one dore, and ye sayd Thomas at ye other Dore: and ye sayd Oneseforus Coming to my bedd side: gave me one dram cupp full of his rum, and my wife another: and ye rest to one of ye garls: (as I think) and then told me of Some Actions that he sayd he saw by them, as he stood upon ye stares: to ye which I sayd I dont believe you: why doe you jest after such a sort, he Answering: againe sayd if you will not believe me ask yor Boye Silvanus for he was in ye Chamber neere to them:, soe ye sayd Oneseforus went out of ye Dore and neere ye Dore taulked with ye sayd Howlong and then they came in, and ye sayd Howlong went to fetch her mare, and when shee had fitted her to goe: called this Deponant out, sayeing Oneseforus had told her of something of unscivellty betwixt her and ye sayd Thomas: but shee sayd shee knew not where it was or not but if it were soe shee woold lay ye fault upon me, staying for mee and my wife to goe with her, I answered her againe shee might have gone home had shee not stayed to write a letter to John pocock, and therefore should not blame mee being not blame worthy: for that woold be hard measure for my Good Will. . ."

DEXTER APPLIES A PLASTER

When the dividing line was finally run in 1712, long after Harris, Williams, Fenner, and Dexter had departed forever from the tumults of town meeting and the clamors of the courts, it was extended only as far west as the Seven Mile Line, where it turned and ran due south to the Warwick north line. This added somewhat to the Pawtuxet tract but it was far short of the great estate of which Harris had dreamed when, in the will he drew just before his second trip to England, he entailed his lands even unto the fourth generation.

One can, naturally, criticize the course pursued by Dexter in this controversy. He obviously used or condoned obstructionist tactics and thereby set a pattern which later Rhode Islanders have followed in causes less worthy than an attempt to prevent a fraud against the Indians. But his arguments in the case and in the Sovereign Plaster are shot through with the fine moral fire of a man fighting for what a tender conscience told him was the right. And no one can accuse him of having "minded more his owne Cabin than the Common Good of our poore tossed Barke & Vessell."[1]

[1] I have made no attempt to document this chapter in detail, but I have not called upon any hitherto unused sources. What I have sought to do was to rewrite the familiar story of the Providence-Pawtuxet land controversies with special emphasis upon the part played in them by Gregory Dexter, deleting those portions, such as the suits against Harrud, Tower, *et al*, which would only confuse the reader if they were included in anything more than the most generalized sort of mention.

Those who wish to examine for themselves the mass of source material which is readily available are referred to *Prov. Recs.*, II, III, V, VI, VIII, XV; *R. I. Col. Recs.*, I and II; *R. I. H. S. Collections*, IX and X, the latter an indispensable source; *R. I. Historical Tracts*, XIV, and 2nd Series, IV; *Mass. Hist. Soc. Proceedings, 2nd Series*, III; *R. I. H. S. Publications*, I; Irving B. Richman, *Rhode Island: Its Making and Its Meaning* (New York and London, 1902), 2 vols.; Chapin, *Documentary History of R. I.*, I; George T. Paine, *A Denial of the Charges of Forgery in connection with the Sachems' Deed to Roger Williams* (Providence, 1896); the Peck MSS. Collection in R. I. H. S.; and the Fenner MSS. Collection in Providence City Hall.

XVI

TWILIGHT YEARS

"SIR," wrote Roger Williams to John Winthrop, Jr., on 19 August 1669, "I have encouraged Mr. Dexter to send you a limestone, and to salute you with this enclosed. He is an intelligent man, a master printer of London, and conscionable (though a Baptist), therefore maligned and traduced by William Harris (a doleful generalist.)

"Sir, if there be any occasion of yourself (or others) to use any of this stone, Mr. Dexter hath a lusty team and lusty sons, and very willing heart, (being a sanguine, cheerful man) to do yourself or any (at your word especially,) service upon my honest and cheap considerations...."[1]

The limestone here referred to by Roger Williams came from Dexter's quarry at Hackleton's Rock, later known as Dexter's Lime Rocks, which lay between the Moshassuck and the Blackstone rivers just east of the present village of Limerock in the town of Lincoln. How early Dexter had acquired this property the records do not reveal. The first mention of the limestone deposit occurs in the records on 27 October 1665, when the town ordered that "those Lime Rockes about Hackletons lime Killne shal be perpetually Common, and that no land shall be laid out on the north East, & south East of the said Kilne within 6 poles, nor upon the other sides, or partes of the said Kilne within 60 poles." Dexter had apparently come into possession of his holdings before this order and had added eighty acres of nearby meadow under the first division of lands within the Seven Mile Line, for on 27 January 1672/3 he deeded all this property to his son Stephen, reserving to his fellow townsmen the right "to fetch for their vse as much lime Rock from the rock Cled Hackeltons Rock as they please" provided they added to the 80 acres sufficient land to compensate for a highway through the land to the rock.[2]

At this site, according to Jonathan Dexter, compiler of the manuscript genealogy of the family, Gregory built his

[1] *Narr. Club Pubs.*, VI, 332.
[2] *Prov. Recs.*, III, 66, 241 and 228-229.

son Stephen a house and planted him an orchard. Only the orchard survived King Philip's War. Stephen Dexter, forced to flee his homestead, took refuge at Field's garrison house in Providence. He died about 1677 and thus Gregory Dexter lost the first of his "lusty sons."[1]

During the war Gregory Dexter had lost his son James, the second-born. In a paper dated 1695, Gregory Dexter says that James died about 19 years earlier, "when I was gone to Long Island."[2] It has always been presumed, therefore, that Gregory Dexter sought a haven on Long Island during the Indian war.

Recently, however, a deed from Gregory Dexter to his son John, in Gregory's handwriting and dated 15 March 1677, has come to light and shows that he was among those who went to the island of Rhode Island during the war. This deed,[3] never before printed, is given here in full:

Providence this 15th of the 1st m. Called March 1677.

This writing sheweth to all people whom it may concern, that I Gregory Dexter (of the Town of Providence, in the Colony of Road-Island and Providence Plantations in New-England being, by the good hand of the Lord preserved in the late war, and now returned from Road-Island, (where I went, in the time of the said war,) to the place of my former abode, in the said Town; and finding my son John Dexter there, who had built a small Cottage for me, & also preparing another building, bigger, intending to erect it in the place of or old ruines, or housing being all burnt by the enemy. And whereas my aforesaid son hath

[1] The manuscript genealogy says Stephen died during the war. All we can say positively is that Gregory Dexter, in a deed dated 15 March 1677 [i. e., 1677/78], refers to his son John as "my only son." Austin, who was not aware of the existence of this deed, which apparently has never been recorded, says Stephen died in 1679. The manuscript genealogy also recounts a tradition that Stephen's son John, of whom the compiler was a grandson, had gone to the old homeplace after the war, dug himself a cave, and lived there all alone for four years. If Austin is correct in his birth date for this John he would have been only four years old when the peace came. It is most likely that Stephen's brother John, rather than his son John, lived in a cave near the Dexter homeplace after the war.

[2] The paper is mentioned by Austin, who does not locate it; it is not to be found among the town records.

[3] In the R. I. Historical Society manuscripts.

bought & sold for me, these divers yeares past, & I have found him faithful therein: Therefore for his incouragement to go forwards to finish the aforesaid building wch he hath begun, & that he may not who is my only Son wander from me in my old age, & for other causes moveing me hereunto: I do declare hereby, That I do give unto my abovesaid Son John Dexter all my Lands & medowes in the Town aforesaid wch I have bought of divers prsons, & my five acre Lot & six acre Lot wch I had of the Town, as also I give unto him, all my little Stock of Cattel that is left, as also all my household goods for him to use, posesse & enjoy, & his heires whilst mortality lasteth Providing, or reserving as followeth: ffirst, That my said Son John / or his heires / shal alow to me & my wife food & rayment convenient, and one bed to lodge on, as also one lowe roome in the said house preparing, whilst we live. And secondly, that he provide or alow food & rayment, with lodging for my two Grand Children, as long as I or my wife doth live, unles we do dispose of them otherwise. And thirdly provided, that if my Daughter Abigael shal marry before I or my wife dy, that my said Son shal alow her such a reasonable portion as we shal advise unto: But if she marry not before I, or my wife dy, that then he or his heires pay unto her out of the said estate given now to him, the full valeu of twenty pounds.

In Testimony of this my act & Deed, I set to my hand & Seale
GREGORY DEXTER

In testimony of my acceptation of my ffathers Deed of gift abovespecified, & upon the provisions expressed, I set to my hand & Seale
JOHN DEXTER

In testimony of my liking of the above Deed of Gift to my Son. & my Sons likeing thereof I consent & set to my hand & Seale
ABIGAILL DEXTER

Those words or his heires, were put in before the sealing

The arrangement established by this deed of gift continued until Gregory's death. On 1 July 1679 Gregory Dexter and his son John were taxed jointly, and thereafter for years their names appeared jointly in the tax lists.

Dexter took steps in March, 1682, to protect the rights of his three fatherless grandchildren—Peleg, Isabel, and James, children of James—to a 10-acre strip of land called Dexter's New Meadow, which lay on the north side of the West River. Gregory had given the land to James when he married, and James had willed it to the children. Now, Dexter charged, Capt. William Hopkins, the surveyor, who had married his son Stephen's widow, had laid out land to Jonathan Whipple which encroached on the ten acres. Whipple had been one of the Pawtuxet Proprietors' supporters in the land disputes, and he and Dexter could still strike sparks when they clashed.[1]

In 1685 Gregory Dexter served his government official-ly for the last time—as a grand juror. From that date his retirement was complete; church and family duties alone were able to engage his attention. By deed of gift in 1696 he provided for his two unmarried grandchildren, Peleg and Isabel. To Peleg he gave his old home lot at the corner of Dexter's Lane and the Towne Street, and ten acres at West River. To Isabel he gave another home lot, next south of the one deeded to Peleg. Both properties were to revert to James, the third grandchild in this branch of the family, if Peleg and Isabel died without issue.[2] These transfers in themselves are of no special interest, but they take on interest when, three years later, on 27 March 1699, Peleg having died, John Dexter, uncle of Peleg and Isabel, quitclaimed to his nephew James all rights in the property —with one exception.

John Dexter reserved "a peece of Ground on the south side of the said southernmost house lot. . . at the place where my Brother James Dexter lieth buried, which shall be two poles long lengthwayes of the said lot and one pole & a halfe wide breadth wayes of the said lot to be for a burieing place for the Dexters who are of the Race of my father the aforesaid Gregory Dexter there to burye their dead if they see cause. . ."[3] This not only locates the ancient Dexter burying ground but the tenor of the language would indicate that the venerable Gregory Dexter was still alive.

This is the last date I can find in Dexter's chronology, and probably he died, as the genealogies state, the ensuing year. His wife Abigail survived him by at least six years. John Dexter, a prominent man in the community—he was

---

[1] For their respective statements, see *Prov. Recs.*, XV, 240, and XVII, 1.

[2] *Prov. Recs.*, XIV, 244-245.

[3] *Prov. Recs.*, IV, 173-174.

deputy for many years, major for the mainland from 1699 to 1705, and Speaker of the House of Deputies in 1704 and 1705—mentions her in his will, dated 15 April 1706. Therein he promised Hannah Sprague ten pieces-of-eight above her wages "if she tarries with my wife and is helpful to my honoured mother during her life."

* * *

The passing of Gregory Dexter removed one of the most controversial figures in Providence history, but he departed in the midst of a strange quiet, for the old fights were over and the town had settled down to a patchwork political peace.

Dexter left it to his children and his grandchildren "to heal the many fold prsant soares" of the town which had been rubbed raw in the days of the land controversy. These descendants followed that wise course pointed out by the gallant Captain Fenner when he took Howlong Harris for his bride. It was a course which for centuries had preserved a modicum of peace among the crowned heads of the world and it worked no less successfully among the humble citizens in the microcosm of Providence Plantations.

Son Stephen, long dead, had married a Whipple, and from the same blood had come the wife of lusty son John. James had married a granddaughter of old William Arnold, the Pawtuxet proprietor. Thereafter such marriages between ancient enemies were to occur with increasing frequency. Grandson John, he who was said to have lived four years alone in a cave, took to wife a daughter of that same Thomas Field who had joined Harris in the suit against Dexter, Fenner, and the Town. John's sister Abigail married Thomas Field, Jr. Other grandchildren, paying little regard to feuds long dead, chose without prejudice from friendly and enemy camps alike, taking unto themselves Whipples, and Olneys, and Fenners.

They left, as the genealogists put it, a numerous posterity.[1]

---

[1] "I have thought," wrote Jonathan Dexter in his manuscript genealogy, "if all the posterity from John, the Grand-Son of Gregory, could be reckoned, it would be as large a number as perhaps could be found from any man that was ever born in America."

TWILIGHT YEARS

Among the descendants of Gregory Dexter are many who have brought honor and gratitude upon the family name. Whenever riches have been their lot in life, and that has been often, they have shared them generously, serving their fellow townsmen, their town, and its institutions as zealously as Gregory Dexter fought the powers of oppression with the printed page in London and, on the fringe of the wilderness, with the divine fire of a tender conscience.

INDEX

INDEX

INDEX

INDEX

INDEX

NOTES ON ILLUSTRATIONS

1. Dexter's signature appears four times—twice in full and twice abbreviated to Gre: Dexter.

3. Page 1, showing block initial A formerly used by Allde. Note that the arms of the E have been chiseled away to transform it into an I. (*Elizabeth Regina* to *Iames Rex*.)

5. Page 1, showing headpiece, actual size of which is 1 x 3 ⅞.

6. Page misnumbered 4, recto of leaf A3. This type was picked up intact as page 3 of Pym's *Speech*.

7. Page 3, which was picked up unchanged from recto of A3 in *A True Copie of the Masterpiece of All those Petitions, etc.*

8. Lines 2 to 6 of the caption title were lifted from Pym's *Speech*, page 3. The ornament is No. 118 in H. R. Plomer, *English Printers' Ornaments*.

9. Page 14, showing the order to print. The headpiece appears frequently in works printed by Oulton and Dexter.

12. Page 3, showing a woodcut and the block of the Seal of the City of London.

15. Fleuron border was used frequently by Oulton and Dexter. Oxford University seal is bogus; cf. McKerrow No. 338.

16. The ornamental block is McKerrow No. 290, used by Edward Allde from 1592 to 1626, and later by Elizabeth Allde and by Richard Oulton.

18. Note that ornament is upside down.

19. The first book about Harvard College, and the first of the Eliot Indian tracts.

20. Cluster of type ornaments is the same as that used on *New Englands First Fruits*.

22. Recto of leaf*٭*٭, showing headpiece and factotum initial block. The latter is upside down. The headpiece appears upside down as headpiece to the introduction in *Queries of Highest Consideration*, by Roger Williams.

24. Page 1, showing headpiece and broken block initial T.

27. Page 1, showing factotum initial block also used in *Mr. Cottons Letter Lately Printed, Examined and Answered*, by Roger Williams.

29. Title page of second edition. Probably not printed by Gregory Dexter.